# Joomla! Search Engine Optimization

Drive people to your site with this supercharged guide to Joomla! and Search Engine Optimization

**Ric Shreves**

BIRMINGHAM - MUMBAI

# Joomla! Search Engine Optimization

First published: July 2012

Production Reference: 1020712

Published by Packt Publishing Ltd.
Livery Place
35 Livery Street
Birmingham B3 2PB, UK.

ISBN 978-1-84951-876-5

www.packtpub.com

Cover Image by John M. Quick (john.m.quick@gmail.com)

# Credits

**Author**

Ric Shreves

**Reviewers**

Herbert-Jan van Dinther

Peter Martin

**Acquisition Editor**

Andrew Duckworth

**Lead Technical Editor**

Andrew Duckworth

**Technical Editor**

Rati Pillai

**Project Coordinator**

Vishal Bodwani

**Proofreader**

Aaron Nash

**Indexers**

Hemangini Bari

Tejal Daruwale

**Production Coordinator**

Prachali Bhiwandkar

**Cover Work**

Prachali Bhiwandkar

# About the Author

**Ric Shreves** is a web applications consultant and tech author. He's been building websites since the mid-90s and writing about tech for almost as long. Ric specializes in open source content management systems and has written texts on each of the big three: WordPress, Joomla!, and Drupal.

Ric is the founding partner of water&stone, a digital agency that focuses on new media and online marketing. He works with clients on digital marketing strategy and supervises the SEO implementation team. Ric lives in Bali, and divides his time between the island and Singapore.

# About the Reviewers

**Herbert-Jan van Dinther** has been working on websites and SEO since 1999. He is currently working as a Senior IT Analyst with a large company. Herbert started website building with Mambo, Joomla!, Drupal, Typo3, and WordPress. He likes to educate people, via several of his websites, on how to use open source content management systems such as WordPress and Joomla!, and how to get them higher in search engines.

He is the author of *Joomla! 1.5 SEO* by Packt Publishing. You can learn more about him on `www.herbertjanvandinther.com`.

> I would like to thank my wife and children for their patience and the time they give me while I am building websites and helping other people.

**Peter Martin** has a keen interest in computers, programming, sharing knowledge, and how people (mis)use information technology. He has a bachelor's degree in Economics (International Marketing Management) and a master's degree in Mass Communication.

He discovered PHP/MySQL in 2003 and Joomla!'s predecessor, Mambo CMS, a year later. Peter has his own business, `www.db8.nl` (founded in 2005), and he supports companies and organizations with Joomla! implementations, support, and Joomla! extension development.

Peter is actively involved in the Joomla! community where he is a member of the Community Leadership Team and Global Moderator at Joomla! forum.

Furthermore, Peter has reviewed the following Packt Publishing books:

- *Joomla! 2.5 Beginner's Guide, Eric Tiggeler*
- *Joomla! 1.6 First Look, Eric Tiggeler*
- *Joomla! 1.5 Templates Cookbook, Richard Carter*

His other interests are open source software, Linux (Debian, Ubuntu, and Arch Linux), plug computers, music (collecting vinyl records), and art house movies. Peter lives in Nijmegen, The Netherlands.

# www.PacktPub.com

## Support files, eBooks, discount offers and more

You might want to visit www.PacktPub.com for support files and downloads related to your book.

Did you know that Packt offers eBook versions of every book published, with PDF and ePub files available? You can upgrade to the eBook version at www.PacktPub.com and as a print book customer, you are entitled to a discount on the eBook copy. Get in touch with us at service@packtpub.com for more details.

At www.PacktPub.com, you can also read a collection of free technical articles, sign up for a range of free newsletters and receive exclusive discounts and offers on Packt books and eBooks.

http://PacktLib.PacktPub.com

Do you need instant solutions to your IT questions? PacktLib is Packt's online digital book library. Here, you can access, read and search across Packt's entire library of books.

## Why Subscribe?

- Fully searchable across every book published by Packt
- Copy and paste, print and bookmark content
- On demand and accessible via web browser

## Free Access for Packt account holders

If you have an account with Packt at www.PacktPub.com, you can use this to access PacktLib today and view nine entirely free books. Simply use your login credentials for immediate access.

# Table of Contents

# Preface

Joomla! is one of the most popular open content management systems. It powers a huge number of today's websites, and is a solid choice for many businesses that want to create a compelling online presence. On today's web, where noise and competition are at their highest levels ever, simply having a great site isn't enough. If you want to be competitive online, you need to have an appreciation for search marketing, and you need fluency with the skills and strategy behind search engine optimization.

Joomla! provides only limited SEO functionality straight out of the box. In this book, we look at how you can create a search engine optimized Joomla! site using a combination of the default Joomla! tools together with a set of popular extensions for the CMS. We also explore in depth the strategy behind SEO and how to set up and prosecute a successful SEO campaign.

Search marketing is a very competitive area, and one that is constantly changing and evolving. SEO skills are in high demand. Use this book to build a solid foundation in SEO and make your Joomla! sites perform to the best of their ability.

## What this book covers

*Chapter 1, An Introduction to Search Engine Optimization*, introduces the key concepts behind search engine optimization, including an explanation of how search engines look at websites and a glossary of terms in common usage in the SEO world.

*Chapter 2, Configuring Joomla!'s SEO Options*, focuses on how to configure Joomla! to achieve optimal SEO advantage. Each of the default SEO features is discussed at length as are server configuration issues.

*Chapter 3, Useful Extensions to Enhance SEO*, reviews the most popular SEO extensions for the Joomla! CMS, then goes on to show the installation and configuration of a sample set of free extensions.

*Chapter 4, Getting Ready for Launch*, is concerned with the soft skills behind SEO, that is, keyword analysis, competitor research, and the development of an SEO keyphrase strategy for a site.

*Chapter 5, Managing SEO on a Live Site*, is concerned with what goes on after the site is launched. The focus is on developing a methodology for continuous improvement, with a look at content strategies, Social Media Optimization, and link building.

# Who this book is for

This book is aimed at site builders, webmasters, and site owners. Advanced technical skills are not required, though the user should be familiar with administering a Joomla! website, including how to install Extensions. If you are concerned with how your Joomla! site ranks on the search engines or with generating traffic for your site, then you will find this book to be of use. The text presumes no existing special knowledge. Basic concepts are explained, as is the thinking behind the approach advocated in this book.

# Conventions

In this book, you will find a number of styles of text that distinguish between different kinds of information. Here are some examples of these styles, and an explanation of their meaning.

Code words in text are shown as follows: "`nofollow` is a possible value for the `rel` attribute inside the `<a>` tag."

**New terms** and **important words** are shown in bold. Words that you see on the screen, in menus or dialog boxes for example, appear in the text like this: "On the right-hand side of the site page is a section named **SEO Settings**, as seen in the next screenshot."

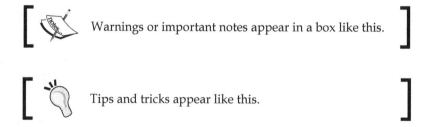

Warnings or important notes appear in a box like this.

Tips and tricks appear like this.

# Reader feedback

Feedback from our readers is always welcome. Let us know what you think about this book—what you liked or may have disliked. Reader feedback is important for us to develop titles that you really get the most out of.

To send us general feedback, simply send an e-mail to feedback@packtpub.com, and mention the book title through the subject of your message.

If there is a topic that you have expertise in and you are interested in either writing or contributing to a book, see our author guide on www.packtpub.com/authors

# Customer support

Now that you are the proud owner of a Packt book, we have a number of things to help you to get the most from your purchase.

# Errata

Although we have taken every care to ensure the accuracy of our content, mistakes do happen. If you find a mistake in one of our books—maybe a mistake in the text or the code—we would be grateful if you would report this to us. By doing so, you can save other readers from frustration and help us improve subsequent versions of this book. If you find any errata, please report them by visiting http://www.packtpub.com/support, selecting your book, clicking on the **errata submission form** link, and entering the details of your errata. Once your errata are verified, your submission will be accepted and the errata will be uploaded to our website, or added to any list of existing errata, under the Errata section of that title.

# Piracy

Piracy of copyright material on the Internet is an ongoing problem across all media. At Packt, we take the protection of our copyright and licenses very seriously. If you come across any illegal copies of our works, in any form, on the Internet, please provide us with the location address or website name immediately so that we can pursue a remedy.

Please contact us at copyright@packtpub.com with a link to the suspected pirated material.

We appreciate your help in protecting our authors, and our ability to bring you valuable content.

# Questions

You can contact us at questions@packtpub.com if you are having a problem with any aspect of the book, and we will do our best to address it.

# 1
# An Introduction to Search Engine Optimization

This chapter lays the foundation for what's to come later in the book. It introduces the basic concepts, terms, and fundamental information needed to understand the rationale behind the techniques discussed in the subsequent chapters. While some of the content in this chapter will be known to experienced users, it will be essential content for newbies and those who are not SEO specialists.

The topics covered in this chapter include:

- An introduction to the SEO process
- An SEO vocabulary
- An explanation of how search engines view your site

## What is SEO?

At the most basic level, **SEO** is an acronym that stands for **Search Engine Optimization**. More importantly, for the purposes of the philosophy espoused in this text, SEO is a process: a series of planning and executing steps that lead to a website being optimized to perform its best on the search engines.

Notice the emphasis on process; SEO is not something you do once and then forget about. While an intensive period of attention to your site's optimization factors can lay a solid foundation and get you off to a proper start, if you do not continue to make efforts to improve your optimization and respond to market conditions, your rankings will erode over time. Moreover, your efforts do not exist in isolation; there are others out there competing for rankings and traffic.

In order to succeed, you need to do your best to stay ahead of the others fighting for ranking for their sites.

 When we talk about search engines in this text, we mean Google, Bing, Baidu, or other similar sites focused on allowing the general public to search for and find information on the web. Typically, what works for one search engine will work for others. Though there are peculiarities and optimization strategies that can be applied to target specific engines, most SEO techniques are search engine agnostic.

The competition for online attention should never be underestimated. If you are in a competitive business vertical, be it travel, finance, gambling, web design, property, or any number of others, the fight for traffic from the search engines is cut-throat. Never forget that the major players out there have dedicated SEO teams that do nothing every day but tweak, optimize, build links, create content, and generally do their best to out-compete all other similar businesses vying for the top spots on the search engines.

In this book, we put forward a methodology for search engine optimization. The process we advocate can be viewed broadly as having two parts: foundations and on-going efforts. We start by looking at how to lay a great foundation for your site, that is, the basics of creating a search engine-friendly site. In later chapters, we turn our attention to on-going techniques for maintaining and improving your rankings over time. Along the way, we look at how to formulate and implement a coherent search engine strategy.

 Never forget, for most site owners the actual goal is traffic generation, not pure search engine ranking.

While many of the issues in SEO relate to technical aspects of the site, there is much more to SEO than just getting the tech right. One of the fundamental principles advocated in this book is to focus on the creation of useful, unique content. There is a strong positive correlation between high quality content and high site ranking. This is one of the few areas where the search engines provide specific guidance about what they are looking for in a site. On the subject of quality, Google provides the following guidance:

- Make pages primarily for users, not for search engines. Don't deceive your users or present different content to search engines than you display to users, which is commonly referred to as "cloaking."

- Avoid tricks intended to improve search engine rankings. A good rule of thumb is whether you'd feel comfortable explaining what you've done to a website that competes with you. Another useful test is to ask, "Does this help my users? Would I do this if search engines didn't exist?"

 For more insights from Google, visit
`http://support.google.com/webmasters/bin/`
`answer.py?hl=en&answer=35769`.

Bing also emphasizes the importance of content and advises as follows:

- Ensure content is built based on keyword research to match content to what users are searching for
- Produce deep, content rich pages; be an authority for users by producing excellent content
- Set a schedule and produce new content frequently
- Be sure content is unique – don't reuse content from other sources

 Don't try to outsmart Google – it's not going to work. Even if you find a way to artificially manipulate your rankings, there will come a day, very soon, when Google will pick up on it and make adjustments to their algorithms. When that happens, your site rankings will plummet and you will go from being a hero to zero.

While content is critical, it should not be your only concern. SEO practitioners often disagree about the relative importance of various factors in site rankings, but there is general agreement on which factors play a part. The search engine business is very competitive, and companies like Google and Bing do not disclose details of how their algorithms work. Fortunately for us, there is a considerable body of third party research focused on discerning trends and patterns in search engine ranking. One of the best sources of information on this topic is *SeoMoz's Search Ranking Factors*, a report they publish free of charge and update annually. The data in the report comes from interviews of more than 130 SEO specialists and from a large data set that seeks to identify correlations between site variables and search engine rank.

 View the report online by visiting `http://www.seomoz.`
`org/article/search-ranking-factors`.

Among the factors that are agreed to be significant are the following:

- Keywords in the domain name
- Keywords in a page's URL
- Keywords in the content title
- Keyword placement on a page
- Keyword repetition on a page
- Uniqueness of content
- Freshness of content
- Facebook activity
- Twitter activity, including influence of account tweeting
- Google+ activity
- Social media up votes and comments
- Click-through rate for the site
- Bounce rate for the site
- Number, quality, and content of links to this site
- Number of internal links
- Number of errors on site
- Speed of site

In sum, the SEO process requires a multifaceted approach. At the most fundamental level, you need to create a site that is search engine-friendly, but in order to excel, you must do more. SEO requires concerted effort across time and you must also focus on the creation of unique, quality content.

**The future of SEO**

SEO is a moving target. The search engines are constantly adjusting their algorithms and practitioners are constantly trying new strategies and modifying their approach. While it is impossible to predict with any accuracy what the future of SEO will bring, there is some consensus among experts about which direction it is moving in. Generally speaking, we believe the future will see a continued emphasis on determining the perceived value of each site. This will be done by looking at not only the quality of the site's content, but also social media signals and site traffic patterns. Site performance will also continue to be a factor, with faster, better built sites being preferred over slow, badly engineered sites.

These factors are consistent with what we know about the general goals the search engines aspire to, that is, to be able to perceive sites more like users perceive them, rather than as a purely mathematical exercise.

# SEO terminology

The SEO field is replete with esoteric terminology and peculiar expressions. An awareness of the discipline's vocabulary is essential for clear understanding. In this section of the chapter, we provide definitions for the most commonly used terms.

# .htaccess

The `.htaccess` file is a Linux configuration file for your Apache web server. In the context of SEO, it is used to help your web server determine how to route HTTP traffic. In the world of SEO, the `.htaccess` file is most commonly discussed in the context of URL aliases for the purpose of creating search engine-friendly URLs.

Note that `.htaccess` is only applicable to sites running on the Apache web server. On Microsoft IIS, the `web.config` file is used to perform similar tasks.

# 301 redirect (also known as Permanent Redirect)

A 301 redirect is an instruction given to the web server, informing it that a page that was previously located at one URL has been moved permanently to a new URL. The 301 redirect is most commonly used in situations where a site has been rebuilt and the URLs have changed. By adding 301 redirects to the site you are able to avoid missed connections caused by traffic going to the old URL. When a 301 redirect is used, the search engines will also update their indexes to remove the old URL for the page and substitute the new one, thereby preserving the page's indexing.

# 302 redirect (also known as Temporary Redirect or Found)

A 302 redirect, like a 301 redirect, informs the web server that a page has been moved. Unlike a 301 redirect, a 302 indicates that the move is temporary. This option is not favored as some search engines will penalize the use of this sort of redirect.

# 404 error (also known as Page Not Found)

When a person visits a URL to a page that no longer exists (or has been moved), or types in an incorrect URL, the visitor will automatically be shown a 404 error message. The default message informs the visitor that the page cannot be found. Many sites build custom pages specifically designed to be displayed when 404 errors occur.

# AdSense

AdSense is a Google advertising program aimed at publishers. Website owners can sign up for the AdSense program and then display advertising on their site (the ad inventory is provided by Google, often from the AdWords program discussed next). The website owner will be paid a percentage of the revenue generated when someone clicks on one of the ads displayed on the site.

# AdWords

AdWords is a Google commercial advertising program aimed at advertisers. If you want to advertise on the Google network, you can sign up for the AdWords program, build an ad, and set a daily budget for the display of that ad. The ad will then appear in the Google network and you will be charged when someone clicks on one of the ads, or according to the number of views.

# Alexa Rank

Alexa.com provides a website ranking service that attempts to rate all the sites on the web in order of their popularity. Like a golf score, the lower the score, the better. The most popular site on the web (typically Google.com) has an Alexa Rank of 1. The service, though not 100% accurate and the subject of some criticism, is yet another way of tracking the success of your efforts to raise your site's profile. To learn more visit `http://alexa.com`.

# Alt attribute

The HTML image tag `<img>` is used to place images on the page. The tag includes an option to specify a value for the attribute `alt`. This attribute is intended to allow webmasters to specify an alternative description for the image, typically for the benefit of users who are using screen readers or browsers with the image display disabled.

# Anchor

Anchors are hyperlinks that allow a user to jump from one place to another within the same page.

# Backlink (also known as Inbound Link)

A backlink is a link on an external site that points to your site.

# Bing Webmaster

The Bing Webmaster service is provided by Microsoft to enable site owners to gain access to some basic tools that help you diagnose and track your site. Registration is free of charge.

# Black hat

Black hat is a label used to describe the use of SEO techniques that are illegal, unethical, or of questionable propriety.

# Bot (also known as robot, spider, or crawler)

A robot, or "bot" for short, is a software agent that indexes web pages. It is also sometimes called a "spider" or a "crawler."

# Canonical URLs

Canonical URLs are URLs that have been standardized into a consistent form. For the search engines, this typically implies making sure all your pages use consistent URL structures, for example, making sure all your URLs start with "www.".

# Cloaking

Cloaking is a black hat SEO technique that involves presenting the search engine spider with different content than you show a normal site visitor.

# Crawl depth

Crawl depth is a measure of how deeply the search engine spider has indexed a website. This is typically an issue relevant for sites with a complex hierarchy of pages. The deeper the spider indexes the site, the better.

# Deep link

Deep link is a hyperlink that points to something other than the front page of a website.

# Doorway page (also known as gateway page)

A doorway page is a page built specifically to point users to another page. This technique is used legitimately when a site owner holds multiple domain names and wishes to channel all the traffic into a primary domain. The technique is often used inappropriately by some black hat SEO practitioners as a way to create highly optimized pages targeting a specific term or terms, then push the users to another site – an online variation of the old bait and switch routine.

# Duplicate content penalty

This is a theory that search engines penalize sites that repeat content, or use content that is duplicated from another source. The theory is controversial, with many believing that the penalty may not exist, or may only be enforced in situations where there are other factors that indicate bad intent.

# Google Webmaster

The Google Webmaster service is provided by Google to enable site owners to gain access to some basic tools that help you diagnose and track your site. Registration is free of charge.

# Internal link density

Internal link density is the number of self-referential links on a site; that is, the number of links on a site pointing to other pages on the same site.

# KEI

**KEI** is an acronym standing for **Keyphrase Effectiveness Index**. The KEI is normally used during key phrase research in an attempt to find the optimal key phrases for a site. It is a simple ratio, most often defined as:

*frequency of search engine queries for the term / number of pages competing for the term*

The more the searches, the more the potential traffic. The lower the competition, the easier it is to rank highly in the SERP. The most ideal term will have low competition and a high number of searches.

# Keyphrase density (also known as keyword density)

Keyphrase density is a calculation done by looking at all the text on a page, then calculating a ratio that represents the total number of words to the number of times a particular key phrase or key word appears on that page.

# Keyword (or keyphrase)

A keyword is a word being targeted for a site's SEO efforts. A keyphrase is simply the targeting of a phrase instead of a single word.

# Keyphrase stuffing

Keyphrase stuffing is the over-optimizing of a page for a particular keyphrase. This is a disfavored practice that can have a negative impact on your site's ranking as it is viewed by the search engines as an attempt to exert inappropriate influence on the rankings for the page.

# Landing page

A landing page is a web page that has been optimized to capture a customer, and is typically used as the target for an ad or other promotional campaign or simply for capturing leads.

# Link building

Link building is the process of seeking out or creating links to a site for the purpose of increasing the site's search engine relevance.

# Link farm

A link farm is a site that includes an excessive number of links. These sites are typically built purely to generate links for SEO purposes. Sites of this nature are disfavored by search engines, which view them as inappropriate attempts to exert influence over rankings.

# Link text (also known as anchor text)

When you create a hyperlink on a page by wrapping a text string with an `<a>` tag, the text wrapped by the tag is referred to as the link, or anchor, text. There is a search engine optimization benefit to using text for hyperlinks, as the text can then be indexed in conjunction with the hyperlink.

# Long tail

In general terms, the long tail of a distribution is the trailing end of the distribution. In the context of SEO, the term is used to refer to targeting longer and more specific search queries, where there is usually less competition.

# Meta tags

Metadata is, quite literally, data about data. On the web, meta tags are the most common implementation of metadata, and in the past they were a key part of search engine indexing. Today, meta tags are still in use on the web and can be found in the head section of web pages.

# MozRank

MozRank is a site ranking algorithm formulated by SeoMoz. It is often used in SEO circles as an alternative to Google's PageRank.

# nofollow

nofollow is a possible value for the rel attribute inside the <a> tag. If the value of the rel attribute for a link is set to nofollow, the search engines' spiders will not follow or index the link.

# Organic rank

Organic rank refers to natural search engine ranking, as opposed to paid ranking.

# Outbound link

Outbound link is a hyperlink on one site pointing to an external site.

# Page rank

Page rank is a ranking algorithm created by, and named for, Larry Page at Google. The ranking criteria are unknown, but the scale ranges from zero at the low end to 10 at the high end. The higher the score, the more persuasive a website is deemed to be. There is an argument, however, that the rank is no longer in use at Google and may not continue to evolve.

# PPC

PPC is an acronym standing for **Pay Per Click** advertising. If you use a PPC advertising scheme, you pay every time someone clicks on one of your ads. The most popular PPC system is the Google AdWords program. It is also sometimes called "pay for performance advertising".

# Reciprocal link

Reciprocal link is a link from one site to another, given in exchange for a link back; a link exchange between webmasters, done in hopes of boosting both sites' rankings.

# Redirect

Redirect is an instruction given to the web server to redirect traffic seeking one URL to a different URL. There are different types of redirects; see 301 redirect and 302 redirect, explained earlier in this chapter.

# Robots.txt

`Robots.txt` is a file containing instructions for search engines' robots. This file is located on the server but is not used by the human visitors to the website.

# SEF URLs

**SEF URLs** is an acronym standing for **Search Engine Friendly URLs**. The term refers to the creation of URLs that use natural words and phrases, rather than query strings and other abstract values (such as numbers) not associated with the page content.

# SEM

**SEM** is an acronym standing for **Search Engine Marketing**. The term is broad, and applies to not only search engine optimization, but also to other techniques, such as social media, pay per click advertising, and other marketing techniques focused on search engines.

# SEOMoz

SEOMoz is a popular commercial SEO consultancy service. Learn more at `http://www.seomoz.org`.

# SERP

**SERP** is an acronym standing for **Search Engine Results Page**.

# SMO

**SMO** is an acronym standing for **Social Media Optimization**. It is the process of using social media to drive traffic to your site and the related process of making your site suitable for social media, for example, by including social bookmarking tools and other social sharing devices on the site's pages.

# Splash page

Splash page is an entry page, typically decorative, used to greet visitors to a website.

# Stop word

These are words included in search queries that are not actively indexed, unless included in quotations (phrase search). Typical examples include articles and conjunctions: the, a, and or.

# White hat

White hat is a label used to describe the use of SEO techniques that are legal, ethical, or exhibit best practices.

# XML site map

XML site maps list the pages on a website in a format that is easily digestible by search engines' agents. The site maps follow a standard convention agreed upon by all the major search engines. The XML site map is typically not visible to site visitors, and should not be confused with the normal site maps often used on the front end of websites.

# How search engines assess sites

Search engines all function in approximately the same fashion: A software agent, known as a bot, a spider, or a crawler, visits a page, gathers the content, and stores it in the search engine's data repository. Once the information is in the repository, it is indexed. The crawling and indexing processes are constant and on-going. Each of the major search engines maintains multiple crawlers that work tirelessly to refresh its index. The spiders find new pages by a variety of methods, typically including XML Site Maps, URLs already in the index, links to pages discovered while indexing, and URLs submitted for inclusion by users. How frequently they visit a specific site, and how deeply they spider the site each visit, varies.

When a user visits the search engine and runs a search, the search engine extracts from the search engine's index a list of pages that are relevant to the query, and then displays that list of pages to the user. The output on the search results page is defined according to each search engine's own criteria. The ranking methodology used by each engine is the result of the search engine's secret algorithm.

The search engine's crawler is primarily interested in certain types of information on the page, particularly the URL, the text, and the links on the page. Formatting is not indexed. Images and other media are indexed by most search engines, but to varying degrees of depth. Some types of media, such as Flash or attached files, are rarely indexed, though there are exceptions.

If you have a Google Webmaster account, you can see a web page exactly as the Googlebot (the name of the Google crawler) sees it. To do this, log into Google Webmaster Tools, and click on a site profile. In the navigation menu on the left-hand side, select the **Diagnostics** menu and then select the **Fetch as Googlebot** option. Type the URL of the page you want to see, and the system will produce the results. You can see in the following screenshots, a webpage, followed by the Googlebot's view of the same page:

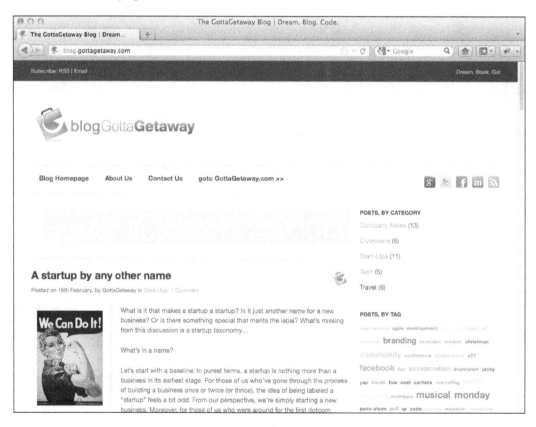

Here's the spider's view of the same page:

# Summary

This chapter is intended to familiarize you with the basic principles of search engine optimization, including the terminology used. As noted at the outset, the philosophy that is promoted in this book focuses on SEO as an on-going process, intended to optimize a website to perform its best on the search engines. Throughout this book, the techniques discussed will all emphasize this process-oriented approach to SEO.

At the conclusion of this chapter you should have gained an awareness of the most commonly used terms in the SEO field, and you should have also gained insights into what is indexed by the search engines and how it is used to produce search engine results. We stated at the beginning of this chapter the importance of quality and original content; at the end of this chapter, where we provided an example of how a search engine spider views your page, you can see again how the content is the key to your efforts.

In the next chapter, we take our first steps towards laying the foundations of SEO for your site, as we look at the default SEO options that are available in your Joomla! site.

# 2
# Configuring Joomla!'s SEO Options

Out of the box, Joomla! includes a number of options that can be configured to provide a basic search engine friendly site, and lays the groundwork for your on-going SEO efforts. In this chapter we look at the default options, what they mean, and how to optimize them. While the default SEO options in Joomla! provide you with basic features you need, such as Search Engine Friendly URLs, this is just the beginning of what you can – and should – do to optimize your site effectively.

The topics covered in this chapter include:

- Creating basic Search Engine Friendly URLs
- Optimizing URLs
- Using URL aliases
- Controlling the title tag
- Creating and optimizing your metadata

## Setting up Search Engine Friendly URLs

Let's start by getting a clear definition of what it means for a site to have Search Engine Friendly URLs.

Sites created with content management systems like Joomla! rely on interaction with the database for the display of content. Accordingly, the URLs often include query strings and other characters that are part of the interaction with the database. A simple HTML site doesn't have this issue; instead, its URLs are typically much simpler and lack the complexity seen in a CMS-powered website.

URLs containing query strings and other odd characters are hard for both humans and search engines to read. Ideal URLs are readable and tell us something about the content of the page. By default, the Joomla! system produces complex URLs containing additional characters that serve no useful purpose for the site visitor. Accordingly, your first step towards making Joomla! more search engine friendly is to get rid of the messy URLs and replace them with **Search Engine Friendly (SEF)** URLs. Let's look at two real examples drawn from the default Joomla! installation (with the sample content loaded) to contrast the differences.

The Joomla! system, with the Search Engine Friendly URLs feature disabled, produces a URL that looks something like the following:

```
http://www.yoursite.com/index.php?option=com_content&view=article&id=
22&Itemid=437
```

That is not search engine friendly. Not only is it hard to read, but also the odd characters and query strings will actually cause problems with some search engines. Moreover, it is simply not human friendly; it is long, hard to remember, and even harder to type accurately.

If you enable Joomla!'s Search Engine Friendly URLs feature, that same page produces a URL that looks something like the following:

```
http://www.yoursite.com/index.php/getting-started
```

This URL is a search engine friendly, and human friendly, URL.

 Joomla! provides two levels of support for the creation of Search Engine Friendly URLs. The most basic level, as seen in the examples above, is enabled by default. A second, more advanced option is custom URL rewriting, which allows you to create URLs that do not include the string `index.php`. Whether the URL rewriting feature is available to you will depend upon the web server being used on your web host.

During installation, Joomla! will automatically enable the SEF URLs option. If the feature has been disabled on your site, you can enable it by following these steps:

1. Access the admin dashboard of your Joomla! site.
2. Click on the shortcut icon labeled **Global Configuration**.
3. On the right-hand side of the site page is a section named **SEO Settings**, as seen in the next screenshot. Set the option **Search Engine Friendly URLs** to **Yes**.

4. Click on the **Save** icon.

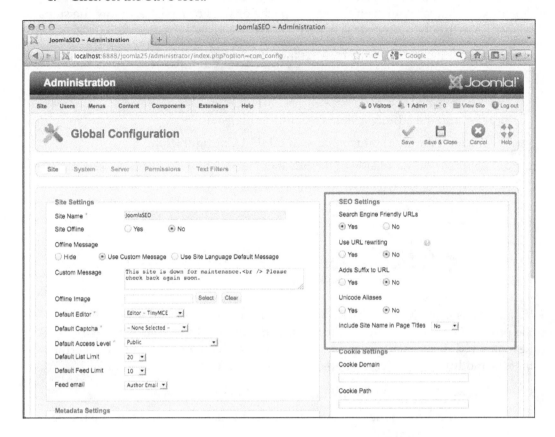

 The current version of Joomla! supports basic SEF URLs without site owners having to worry whether their web server meets special requirements. If you want to do more, however, you will need to pay attention to your web server, as discussed next.

With the **Search Engine Friendly URLs** option enabled, you will have basic SEF URLs for your site. However, if possible, you will want to do more. URL rewriting will allow you to create superior URLs, without the index.php string included in all the URLs.

In other words, instead of getting the following URL:

http://www.yoursite.com/index.php/getting-started

When the URL rewriting feature is enabled, you will get the following URL:

http://www.yoursite.com/getting-started

To enable URL rewriting, you will need to take additional steps. The exact steps depend on whether your web server is Apache or IIS. For Apache, follow the steps below (IIS instructions appear later):

1. Access the files of your Joomla! installation on the server.

2. Find the file `htaccess.txt`. Create a duplicate of it and rename the new file to `.htaccess`.

3. Log into the admin system of your Joomla! site.

4. Click on the shortcut icon labeled **Global Configuration**.

5. On the right-hand side of the Site page is a section named **SEO Settings**.

6. Set the **Use URL Rewriting** option to **Yes**.

7. Click on the **Save** icon.

 You must use the `.htaccess` file provided by Joomla! Do not attempt to create your own or modify the file, unless you have experience with this process.

If your site is using Microsoft's IIS Web server, instead of the Apache Web server, the process is different. Before you get started, you must make sure that the IIS URL Rewrite Module is installed on the server and is activated. Once you have verified that the module is installed and enabled, follow these steps for IIS Version 7:

1. Access the files of your Joomla! installation on the server.

2. Find the file `web.config.txt`. Create a duplicate of it and rename the new file to `web.config`.

3. Log into the admin system of your Joomla! site.

4. Click on the shortcut icon labeled **Global Configuration**.

5. On the right-hand side of the Site page is a section named **SEO Settings**.

6. Set the **Use URL Rewriting** option to **Yes**.

7. Click on the **Save** icon.

 The Joomla! SEF URLs functionality is enabled by a Joomla! plugin named System - SEF. This plugin must be enabled for SEF URLs to work. Although it is enabled by default, if you are having problems getting the Search Engine Friendly URLs functionality to work on your site, visit the Plugin Manager (located under the Extensions menu) and assure the plugin is enabled in your system.

# Configuring URL aliases

The Joomla! Global Configuration Manager provides you with several options that enable you to create more effective URLs. There are two options to consider; they may not both be right for you, so it's important to understand their implications. The two options relate to whether your URL uses a suffix and whether the URL alias is in Unicode.

Both of the URL configuration options are located in the SEO Settings section of the Configuration Manager and can be seen in the image included in the section immediately above.

The first option to consider is whether you want your URLs to include a suffix. The suffix will be supplied automatically by the system and will reflect the document type. This will result in the system adding `.html` to the end of the URL. In other words, instead of getting the following URL:

`http://www.yoursite.com/getting-started`

When this feature is enabled, you will get the following URL:

`http://www.yoursite.com/getting-started.html`

To enable this option for your site, follow these steps:

1.  Go to the admin dashboard of your Joomla! site.
2.  Click on the shortcut icon labeled **Global Configuration**.
3.  On the right-hand side of the Site page is a section named **SEO Settings**, as seen in the previous screenshot. Set the option **Adds Suffix to URLs** to **Yes**.
4.  Click on the **Save** icon.

> Is there an advantage to be gained by adding a suffix to your URLs? Probably not. There's little evidence to support the idea that there is a difference as far as the search engines are concerned. For your users, it's just another chance to make a mistake when typing in the URL.

> Note that it is also possible to change the default suffix from `.html` to `.htm`, though it does require editing one of the Joomla! core files - changes that might get lost the next time the core files are updated. If you really want to do this, read the information found at `http://docs.joomla.org/SEO`.

If your site is likely to use non-standard or non-English characters in your URL aliases, you will want to activate the Unicode option. If you do not enable the Unicode option, the system will attempt to transliterate any non-Latin characters in the alias into a standard Latin character.

> Note that some e-mail clients do not support UTF8, so if your target markets are purely in the Americas, or you otherwise are not interested in supporting foreign languages, you should pass on the Unicode option.

To enable this option for your site, follow these steps:

1. Go to the admin dashboard of your Joomla! site.
2. Click on the shortcut icon labeled **Global Configuration**.
3. On the right-hand side of the Site page is a section named **SEO Settings**, as seen in the previous screenshot. Set the option **Unicode Aliases** to **Yes**.
4. Click on the **Save** icon.

> Check out *Chapter 3, Useful Extensions to Enhance SEO*, for a discussion of extensions that can further optimize your URLs.

# Creating URL aliases for your articles

Assuming you have set the system to use SEF URLs, as described above, Joomla! will automatically create the URL aliases for your content items. The automatic aliases are based on the article's title, and may not always be optimal for your site. While the default aliases may be fine for many people, if you are concerned about competitive SEO, you will want to exercise your own control over the aliases. Fortunately, Joomla! makes it possible for you to specify your own URL aliases.

> Unlike some other systems, like WordPress and Drupal, it is not possible to set up a formula that will automatically create aliases according to your specifications. In Joomla!, you will have to create them manually for individual pages or menu items.

The alias can be created either at the time the item is created or later. There are two possible avenues for setting the alias, though both may not be available, depending on the nature of the page's contents.

Note that it's best to set your aliases at the time you publish the page. If you change the alias subsequent to the publication of the item, you run the risk of breaking links to the existing page and creating errors. If you must change the alias after the page has been live, you will want to create a 301 redirect to make sure that you do not lose traffic to the page or indexing of that page on the search engines.

If the page contains an article, the most obvious place for setting the URL alias is inside the **Article Manager**. As you can see in the next screenshot, the **Edit Article** (and **Add New Article**) page includes a field clearly labeled **Alias**. Changing the value of the **Alias** field will change the URL alias for the article.

Note that using spaces in your alias is not recommended. If you want to force a visual break between words, the best course is to use the hyphen character '-'.

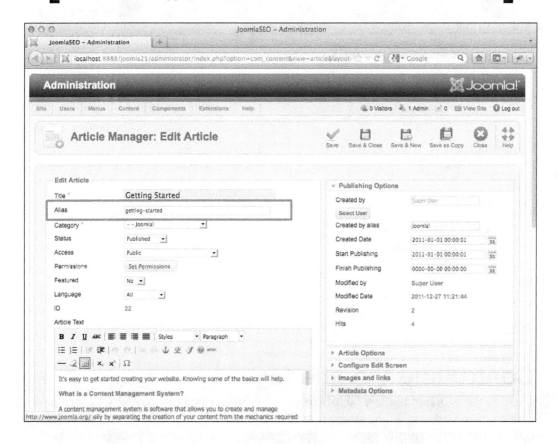

The second option for controlling the URL alias is only available where the page is linked to a menu. If the page is available via one of the Joomla! menus, you can manage the URL alias via the **Menu Manager**.

As you can see in the next screenshot, the **Edit Menu Item** (and **Add Menu Item**) page includes a field labeled **Alias**. Changing the value of this field will change the URL alias for the menu item.

If you wish to modify the URL alias associated with a Joomla! component, the **Menu Manager** provides you with your only option for modifying the alias.

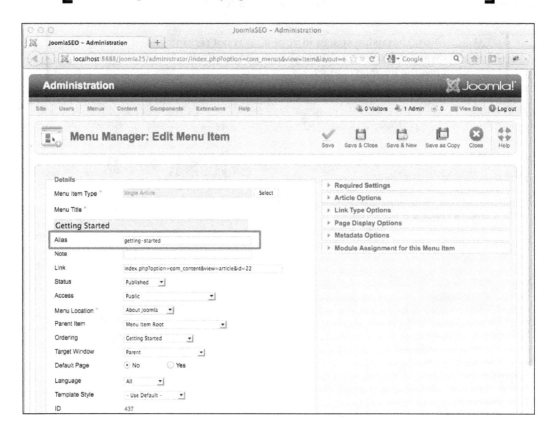

# Controlling the title tag

The title tag is one of the key factors in your SEO success; indeed, many experts will single out the title tag as the single most important factor in SEO. If you ignore the optimization opportunity presented here, you are missing one of your best chances for gaining search engine rank and traffic from the search engines.

To begin, let's define what we're talking about when we refer to the title tag. In the context of SEO, we're talking about the contents of the `<title>` tag, which is located in the head of the HTML document, as you can see in the next screenshot; the `<title>` tag is highlighted in this screenshot of the source code for the default Joomla! "Getting Started" page. The title tag is often referred to as the page title, but be careful not to confuse this with the article title, which appears at the top of a page containing article text.

```
<!DOCTYPE html PUBLIC "-//W3C//DTD XHTML 1.0 Transitional//EN" "http://www.w3.org/TR/xhtml1/DTD/xhtml1-transitional.dtd">
<html xmlns="http://www.w3.org/1999/xhtml" xml:lang="en-gb" lang="en-gb" dir="ltr" >
    <head>
        <base href="http://                    /index.php/getting-started" />
    <meta http-equiv="content-type" content="text/html; charset=utf-8" />
    <meta name="author" content="Super User" />
    <meta name="generator" content="Joomla! - Open Source Content Management" />
    <title>Getting Started</title>
    <link href="/joomla25/templates/beez 20/favicon.ico" rel="shortcut icon" type="image/vnd.microsoft.icon" />
```

The title tag serves multiple important functions. First, the value given in this tag shows up on the browser title bar, and if the browser supports tabs, it typically also appears as the label for the tab, as seen in the next screenshot:

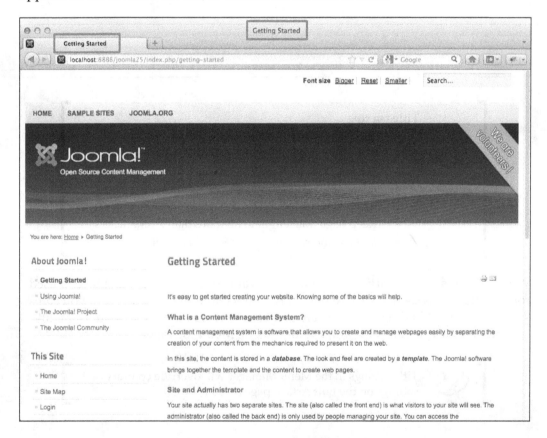

Finally, and most importantly for your SEO efforts, the title tag is shown on the SERP listing for your page, as seen in the next screenshot:

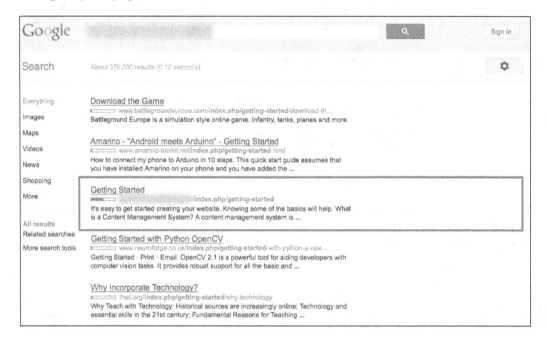

**Title tag tips**

- Use key phrases in your page titles
- The title should reflect the page contents
- Start the title with the key phrase
- Don't over-optimize the title by trying to cram in too many keywords
- Keep page title length to no more than 70 characters
- Make it compelling for users to click on it

When you create a new article in Joomla!, the value entered in the **Title** field is used for the title tag, as seen in the previous screenshots. In the next screenshot you can see the **Title** field highlighted; the value entered in this field will be used as the title tag for the article, absent a contrary setting in the Menu Manager.

Title settings in the Menu Manager will override contrary settings on the Edit Article page.

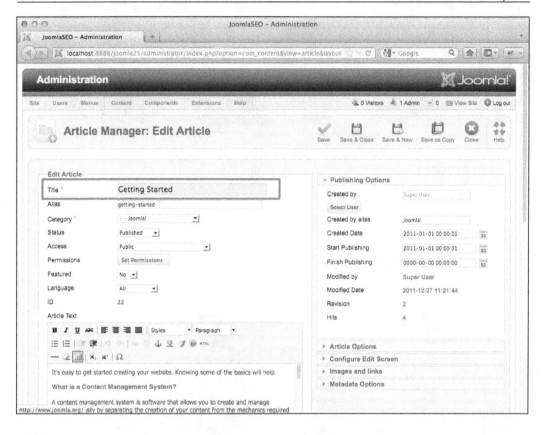

# Article title vs. page title (title tag)

Don't be confused by the language used in Joomla! The value of the **Title** field can also appear on the screen as the title for the article itself – immediately above the body of the article – but it does not have to work that way. If you want your SEO page title (that is, the one that appears at the top of the browser) to be different than the title that appears at the beginning of the article, you can do so.

To set this up, you have to set the **Show Title** option to **Hide**, then create a separate title inside the body of the article. To change the **Show Title** option, click on the **Article Options** heading in the right-hand side column of the **Edit Article** page, as shown in the next screenshot. Set the combo box by the option **Show Title** to **Hide** and then click on **Save**:

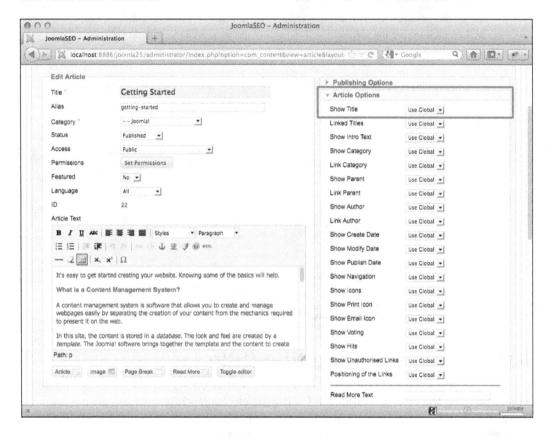

At this point, the value entered in the Title field will only show in the browser, but not at the top of the body of the article. To add a title heading to the top of your article, you will need to enter it into the first line of the **Article Text** editing box, and style it so that it looks appropriate for an article title.

Note that there is another option available to you to achieve this result: If the article is also a **Menu Item**, you can use the **Menu Title** field to control the page title, without affecting the article title, as explained next.

A second choice for managing the title tag is available through the **Menu Manager**. As seen in the next screenshot, the **Edit Menu Item** page (and the **Add Menu Item** page) includes a field labeled **Menu Title**. The **Menu Title** field controls the label for the item that appears on the menu; it also controls the title tag:

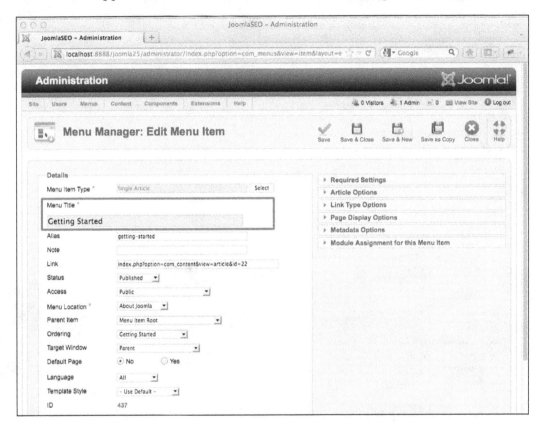

 Settings in the **Menu Manager** will override settings in the **Article Manager**.

Another option preferred by some owners is to include the site name in the title tag. Joomla! makes this easy to do. To include your site name in the page titles, follow these steps:

1. Go to the admin dashboard of your Joomla! site.

2. Click on the shortcut icon labeled **Global Configuration**.

3. On the right-hand side of the site page is a section named **SEO Settings**, as seen in the next screenshot. Next to the label **Include Site Name in Page Titles** is a combo box; select either **After** or **Before**.

4. Click on the **Save** icon.

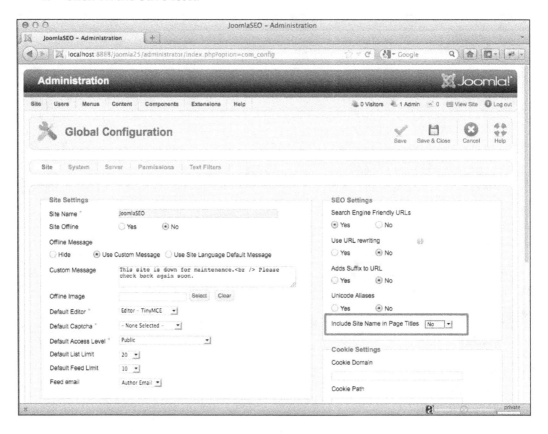

Depending on your selection, the site's name will now appear as part of the page title string, either before, or after the page-specific title string. Generally speaking, you will want to put the page-specific title string first, as this will be displayed when the page shows up in the SERPs. The only exception is the home page, where the site name is logically placed first in the order.

 To customize your site name, use the **Site Name** field (visible in the left-hand side column in the previous screenshot) in the **Global Configuration** manager.

In *Chapter 3, Useful Extensions to Enhance SEO*, we also discuss extensions that can be used to enhance your management of the title tag.

# Managing metadata

Metadata is used to describe the contents of a page. In the past, metadata played a key role in helping search engines understand the nature and content of pages, but today it plays a less critical role. Despite its decreasing importance, metadata should never be ignored; it is the one technical feature of pages that is purely intended to help understand and categorize the page content and therefore should always be used to further your SEO goals.

Metadata is added to pages through the use of meta tags, which appear in the head of the HTML document. While the W3C metadata standards provide for a wide range of possible meta tags, Joomla! only gives us easy access to a subset of the standard. The tags available through Joomla! are shown in the following table:

| Joomla! label | Meta tag | Notes | Importance |
|---|---|---|---|
| Description | `meta name="description"` | Should describe the content of the page. Note that this tag is important as some search engines display this as the description of the link when it appears on the SERP. That also means you should make sure it is grammatically correct and uses proper punctuation. | High |
| Keywords | `meta name="keywords"` | Lists the keywords and phrases you are targeting for the page. | Medium |

| Joomla! label | Meta tag | Notes | Importance |
| --- | --- | --- | --- |
| Robots | `meta name="robots"` | A substitute for the `robots.txt` file in terms of providing the search engines with instructions about what to index on your site.<br><br>Your choices here are limited to:<br><br>• Index, Follow<br>• No index, Follow<br>• Index, No follow<br>• No index, No follow | Medium |
| Author | `meta name="author"` | Intended to contain the author of the HTML page and provide contact information. | Low |
| Content Rights | `meta name="rights"` | Used to declare the ownership rights of the intellectual property on the page and its terms of use. Use this as an alternative to displaying a copyright message directly on your pages. | Low |
| External Reference | `meta name="xreference"` | Add a link to a citation or related external resource. | Low |
| Generator | `meta name="generator"` | Declares the name and version number of the publishing tool used to create the page. This is set automatically by Joomla! and cannot be controlled without hacking the core or modifying the template's `index.php` file. | Low |

The next screenshot shows what the meta tags look like in the head of a document; in this case we have simply populated each field with a descriptive label – you would never use this content on a live site!

```
⊙ ○ ○              Source of: http://localhost:8888/joomla25/index.php/getting-started
<!DOCTYPE html PUBLIC "-//W3C//DTD XHTML 1.0 Transitional//EN" "http://www.w3.org/TR/xhtml1
/DTD/xhtml1-transitional.dtd">
<html xmlns="http://www.w3.org/1999/xhtml" xml:lang="en-gb" lang="en-gb" dir="ltr" >
        <head>
              <base href="http://localhost:8888/joomla25/index.php/getting-started" />
   <meta http-equiv content-type content text/html; charset=utf-8 />
   <meta name="keywords" content="This is the output of the Site Meta Keywords field." />
   <meta name="rights" content="This is the output of the Content Rights field." />
   <meta name="author" content="This is the Author field, from the Article page." />
   <meta name="robots" content="index, follow" />
   <meta name="description" content="This is the output of the Site Meta Description field." />
   <meta name="generator" content="Joomla! - Open Source Content Management" />
   <title>Getting Started</title>
   <link href="/joomla25/templates/beez_20/favicon.ico" rel="shortcut icon"
type="image/vnd.microsoft.icon" />
   <link href="http://localhost:8888/joomla25/index.php/component/search/?Itemid=437&
amp;format=opensearch" rel="search" title="Search JoomlaSEO"
type="application/opensearchdescription+xml" />
   <script src="/joomla25/media/system/js/mootools-core.js" type="text/javascript"></script>
   <script src="/joomla25/media/system/js/core.js" type="text/javascript"></script>
Line 14, Col 85
```

In Joomla!, metadata can be set globally for the entire site, and individually for specific pages. Where there is no information provided for a specific page, the global metadata will be used. The best practice is to populate the global metadata with information relevant to your site as a whole, then add your page-specific metadata to describe the contents of individual pages.

> On this point there is some debate. While we recommend setting global metadata which can be used as the default value, there is also merit to leaving this blank, as most of the major search engines will then try to extract this information from the page content. In theory, allowing the search engine to extract page-relevant data is better than having a number of pages with identical meta content. The problem is that you lose all control if you leave it in the hands of the search engine. Moreover, the effectiveness of the search engine's efforts will depend on how your content is structured; if meaningful content is buried, what the search engine extracts may not be optimal.

To set your global metadata, follow these steps:

1. Go to the admin dashboard of your Joomla! site.

2. Click on the shortcut icon labeled **Global Configuration**.

3. On the left-hand side of the site page is a section named **Metadata Settings**, as seen in the next screenshot. Add your site description and keywords to the fields of the same.

4. If you are not using a `robots.txt` file, enter a value for the **Robots** field.

5. If you wish to assert rights to the intellectual property on the site, add that information to the **Content Rights** field.

6. If you wish to use the meta author field for your content items, set **Show Author Meta Tag** to **Yes**.

7. Click on the **Save** icon.

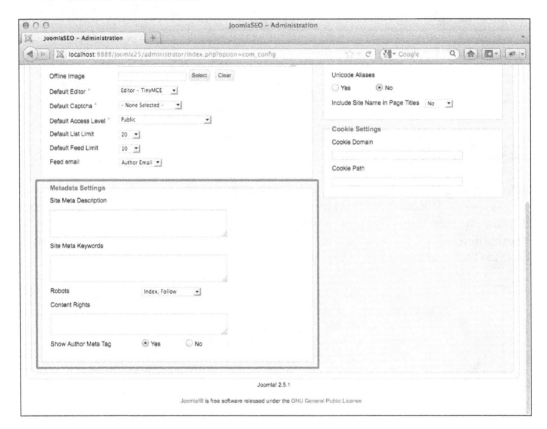

**How long is too long?**

While there aren't any clear maximum lengths for the data strings you put into your meta tags, there are some recommended lengths to keep in mind:

- Title: 60 - 70 characters (Google & Bing display 69 characters in the SERP)

- Description: 150 - 160 characters (Google displays 156 characters in the SERP; Bing, 150)

- Keywords: 256 characters

When you create, or edit, an article, you will have the opportunity to specify metadata for that particular page. If you input data into the article **Metadata Options**, it will override the global metadata for the site, at least for that particular page.

To set the metadata for a specific article, simply open the **Edit Article** page, as shown in the next screenshot, and click on the **Metadata Options** label in the right-hand side column. The metadata fields will unfold, allowing you to create **Meta Description**, **Meta Keywords**, **Robots**, **Author**, and **Content Rights** values for this particular page.

>  Note there's also an extra field here: **External Reference**. This field allows you to add a citation, source, or other relevant link that will appear in the meta data for this item. The meta field used is `meta name="xreference"`.

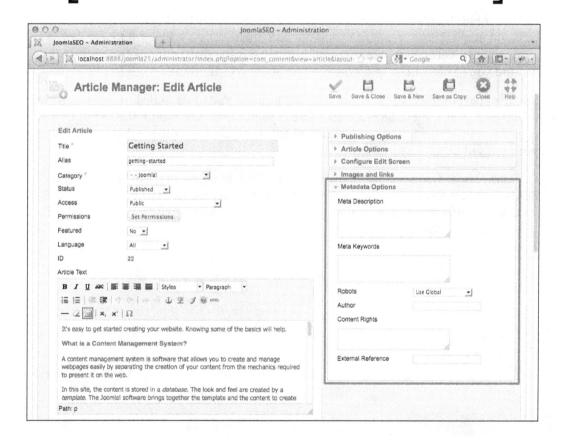

In terms of SEO strategy, you should always strive to provide specific metadata for individual pages. Simply using the global metadata throughout the site is not optimal and causes you to miss opportunities.

# Summary

This chapter covers the basic SEO-related configuration options inside the default Joomla! installation. At the end of this chapter, you should be able to set up Search Engine Friendly URLs and optimize to the extent permitted by the default Joomla! system. SEF URLs are a necessity and you should complete this task before going any further in this book.

Other content in this chapter focuses on how to create URL aliases for specific pages or menu items. This is a useful technique and one that you will want to use if SEO is a priority for your site. Make sure you understand the distinction between the title tag and your article titles and how to control them individually.

The final part of the chapter deals with the topic of metadata and shows you how to set up both global metadata and individual page metadata. Again, this is important if SEO is a priority for you, and you need to understand how to set the metadata for your individual articles.

Looking forward, in the next chapter we discuss extensions that can enhance your SEO efforts. Some of these extensions provide improvements over the basic system's functions, while others add completely new options. Finding the right mix is the key to your SEO success with Joomla!

# 3
# Useful Extensions to Enhance SEO

One of the clear advantages of the Joomla! system is the existence of a large number of extensions that can be plugged in to expand the functionality of the default system. A number of these extensions are designed to enhance your ability to achieve search engine optimization. Like the extensions in other categories, the SEO extensions are of varying functionality and quality. In this chapter, we look at a number of the SEO extensions with the goal of helping you understand exactly what they can do and why you might want to consider adding them to your Joomla! site.

We then show you how to install a set of non-commercial extensions that will allow you to achieve improved SEO for your site.

Topics covered in this chapter include:

- How to find extensions for your Joomla! site
- Our list of the top ten SEO-related extensions for Joomla! 2.5
- How to install and configure common SEO extensions

 Note that the extensions in this chapter are all compatible with version 2.5.x of Joomla!. Most also offer versions compatible with older Joomla! releases.

# Finding SEO modules

While you can always visit Google and run a search for Joomla! SEO extensions, there's a better way to find modules and components for your Joomla! site. The Joomla! community maintains a large directory of extensions specifically for the CMS at `http://extensions.joomla.org`.

The **Joomla! Extensions Directory** (also known as **JED**) is a great starting point for finding useful extensions. The directory includes a description, contact information, user reviews, and information about the compatibility of each extension. Though you are not able to download extensions from the site, you can at least browse listings by topic, and get a good idea of the various options that are open to you. Some extensions overlap with others, some are free, some are not. Accordingly, your first step should be to look at a number of extensions and decide what combination of extensions is most suitable for your site.

> Always check carefully the compatibility of the extensions. Extensions created for older versions of Joomla! are unlikely to work properly with newer version of the system.

# Top SEO modules for Joomla!

The extensions discussed in this chapter take a variety of forms. Some are components, some are modules, and some are plugins, with many being combinations of these things bundled into one. The exact nature of the extension – that is, whether it is a component, module, or plugin – is really of little importance to you as an SEO practitioner. What is important is the functionality the extension delivers.

The extensions listed next provide a range of functionality. Some of the extensions are designed to do only one thing; others are complex extensions that provide a surprising number of features. What is right for you is a personal decision. You should always try to only install things you will use; the argument being that you should favor simpler and more narrowly tailored solutions. However, you also need to consider the added overhead that comes from having multiple extensions installed. If you choose a single extension that can do a number of things, you may need to install fewer extensions in total, thereby decreasing maintenance in the future.

> The extensions that are listed next are presented in alphabetical order, along with the links to download them. Some are free of charge, others are commercial and require a fee or subscription.

# AceSEF

`http://extensions.joomla.org/extensions/site-management/sef/10019`

AceSEF provides SEF URLs and metadata generation. The extension is similar to and competes with sh404SEF (described later on in this chapter), but unlike sh404SEF, AceSEF offers the basic edition free of charge. The basic edition provides only the SEF URL and metadata tools; the premium editions include additional features, including site maps and social bookmark integration. Note that you must register to download this extension.

## Advanced Title Manager

`http://extensions.joomla.org/extensions/site-management/seo-a-metadata/title-management/11826`

Advanced Title Manager improves on the title management functionality in the Joomla! core. The extension allows you more control over the title tag, and lets you create patterns that automatically construct the title string according to your criteria. The system even allows you to specify multiple patterns that will be applied depending upon context, allowing you to use different patterns in different situations. This is a commercial extension.

## Easy Frontend SEO

`http://extensions.joomla.org/extensions/site-management/seo-a-metadata/17926`

Like several others mentioned in this chapter, this extension gives you control over your site metadata. Unlike most of the others, this does it from the frontend of your website. With this extension installed, you can edit your metadata fields while viewing the pages on the frontend of the website, instead of from the administration system. Title tag management is also possible. This is a non-commercial extension.

## Facebook-Twitter-Google+1

`http://extensions.joomla.org/extensions/social-web/social-share/social-multi-share/18072`

This extension adds buttons that allow users to cross-post your content to Twitter, Facebook, and Google+. It also supports the Facebook comments functionality, giving you easy-to-use threaded comment functionality with a social twist. Note that to use this extension to its fullest, you will need to have accounts on the various services and you will need to set up a Facebook application to be used by the extension. This is a non-commercial extension.

# iJoomla SEO

`http://seo.ijoomla.com/`

iJoomla SEO is an all-in-one SEO component. It includes a large number of tools and does about everything except SEF URLs. This extension targets the do-it-yourselfer who wants to manage their site SEO themselves and it includes access to a number of SEO tutorial videos. Among the tasks it accomplishes are: metadata management, redirects, keyword optimization guides, keyword rank monitoring, and automatic addition of Alt tags. iJoomla SEO is a commercial extension.

# JoomSEF

`http://extensions.joomla.org/extensions/site-management/sef/1063`

JoomSEF is a full-featured SEO management tool for Joomla!. Despite the name, the extension offers much more than Search Engine Friendly URLs; it also provides metadata management, sitemap generation, redirect management, custom 404 pages, and more. The free version contains all the features of the commercial version, but includes a link back to the author's site.

# Nice Social Bookmark

`http://extensions.joomla.org/extensions/social-web/social-share/social-multi-share/10676`

Nice Social Bookmark provides your site with a very complete set of social bookmarking buttons. The extension includes integration for 13 of the most popular services, including Facebook, Twitter, Digg, and Google+. The extension includes a number of options for controlling the position and styling of the icons. You can also select the pages where you want the buttons to appear. This is a non-commercial extension.

# obRSS

`http://extensions.joomla.org/extensions/content-sharing/rss-syndicate/6233`

The obRSS extension adds advanced RSS feed management to your site. The extension allows you to create multiple RSS feeds and customize them individually, or you can merge multiple feeds into one master feed. Feedburner integration is also supported, giving you the option to tap into the power of Google's Feedburner service. This is a commercial extension.

# RSSeo Suite

`http://www.rsjoomla.com/joomla-extensions/joomla-seo-sef.html`

The RSSeo Suite is an "SEO-assistant" type of application; that is, it provides a wide variety of metrics, tools, and tips. It's designed for the site owner who wants to take the do-it-yourself approach to SEO for their site. The extension includes an SEO dashboard that provides you with access to Google, Alexa, Bing, and Compete date inside your administration interface. The extension provides metadata and title management, and can also "grade" your pages and provide you with recommendations for improvements. RSSeo Suite is a commercial extension.

# SEO Canonicalisation Plugin

`http://extensions.joomla.org/extensions/site-management/seo-a-metadata/5355`

A simple extension that does only one thing: allows you to set your preferred canonicalisation form for your URLs and then enforces it across the site. This is a non-commercial extension.

# SEO Friendly Links and Images

`http://extensions.joomla.org/extensions/site-management/seo-a-metadata/alt-text/19121`

Out of the box, Joomla! doesn't provide the ability to easily control the `alt` and `title` attributes for links and images. The SEO Friendly Links and Images extension fills the gap in the Joomla! system. With the extension installed and enabled, `title` and `alt` attributes are set automatically, based on the link text or the image name. The administrator can also override the automatic values to specify exactly what is wanted. The extension is non-commercial.

# SEO-Generator

http://extensions.joomla.org/extensions/site-management/seo-a-metadata/meta-data/7171

The SEO-Generator is an automated metadata generator for your Joomla! site. While it is generally better to manually tailor the metadata of each article to your content and your SEO goals, the SEO-Generator extension uses a better-than-average approach to automatic creation. It works by identifying the most commonly used words in the article, removes common parts of speech and other words you have included in a blacklist, and then adds the top words to the keywords field for the article. It also gives you the ability to set title configurations, robots meta tags, and Google Webmaster verification tags. This is a commercial extension.

# SEO Links Pro

http://3dwebdesign.org/en/seo-links-pro-joomla

The SEO Links Pro extension automates the creation of links on the keywords and phrases that appear in the articles on your site. You can set up the extension to automatically add internal or external links to the words you select. You can also cap the number of times links are generated, and set other variables that help prevent irrelevant or excessive link building. The extension is commercial.

# SEOSimple

http://extensions.joomla.org/extensions/4102/details

The SEOSimple extension provides automatic population of your site's meta description tag. It does this by grabbing a pre-defined length of text from the start of the article and using it for the description field. Additionally, the extension allows you to automatically set your page title tag. This is a non-commercial extension.

# sh404SEF

http://anything-digital.com/sh404sef/seo-analytics-and-security-for-joomla.html

The primary feature of this extension is the ability to easily and efficiently generate Search Engine Friendly URLs. The extension improves on Joomla!'s default SEF URL functionality by giving you more control over the URLs, by generating SEF URLs for your component paths, and for reducing the possibility of duplicate content on your site (a situation produced by Joomla!'s failure to block access to the original URL when it creates a URL alias).

This extension has been around for a while and over the years it has grown in functionality. The newest version also includes Google Analytics integration, a short URLs feature, and the ability to add social sharing tools to your content. The extension also provides management for titles and some meta tags. sh404SEF is a commercial extension.

## Ultimate Site Tools

```
http://extensions.joomla.org/extensions/site-management/seo-a-
metadata/site-verification/18872
```

The Ultimate Site Tools extension rolls 13 different SEO-related tools into one package. What it lacks in depth, it certainly makes up for in breadth. Among the key features are title management, canonical URLs, site verification codes, an HTML optimizer, and email cloaking. This is a commercial extension.

## Xmap

```
http://joomla.vargas.co.cr/en/downloads/components/xmap
```

Xmap is a site map generator component for Joomla!. The extension allows to automatically generate XML site maps, based upon the menu structure of your site. Configuration options let you select which items to include or exclude as well as the ability to set priority among them. This extension is non-commercial.

# Installing and configuring common SEO modules

In the following section of this chapter, we're going to look at how you can achieve a number of key SEO optimization goals through the installation and configuration of a set of extensions. All of the extensions discussed are non-commercial and are available through the Joomla! extensions directory.

Taken together, the extensions listed will achieve the following enhancements to your site:

- Improved metadata management
- Improved title tag management
- Canonical URLs
- Creation of an XML site map

- Management of `alt` and `title` attributes
- Implementation of social cross-posting
- Implementation of social bookmarking tools for your site visitors

If you implement these extensions, and also take full advantage of the SEF URLs functionality in the Joomla! core, you will be well on your way to having your site on solid SEO footing.

 There are several extensions, discussed earlier, that provide a number of these options inside of one single package. Those packages, however, are commercial. If you want to install and use one of those packages, you can, but you will need to pay for it (or, in the case of the JoomSEF extension, you can get it for free, but you need to display a link back to the developer).

# Implementing metadata management

While the default Joomla! installation provides some options for metadata management, there are several extensions that provide improved access and control to the meta and title fields. One of the friendliest of the options is the Easy Frontend SEO extension. The extension is free of charge and gives you the ability to browse the front end of your site and update your meta fields while viewing the content item, a nice improvement over the standard Joomla! metadata administration scheme.

To set this up, follow these steps:

1. Download and install the East Frontend SEO extension, discussed earlier.
2. Access the **Plugin Manager** and find the plugin named **System – Easy Frontend SEO**. Click on it to open the editing screen for the plugin.
3. Change the **Status** to **Enabled**.
4. In the **Basic Options** column on the right-hand side, select any configuration options you wish to modify.
5. Open the **Advanced Options** pane to see your choices for display of the Easy Frontend SEO controls on the site. The default view is a modal window, but you can also set the extension to use a toolbar instead.
6. Click on **Save & Close**.

Once the extension is enabled, visit the frontend of your website. If you are logged in as the admin super user, you will see at the top right-hand side of the pages a rectangular box with a series of green checkmarks in it. Click on the checkmarks and a light box-type window (that is, a "modal window") will pop up, showing the title and meta fields for that page. You can see in the next screenshot, what that might look like on your site:

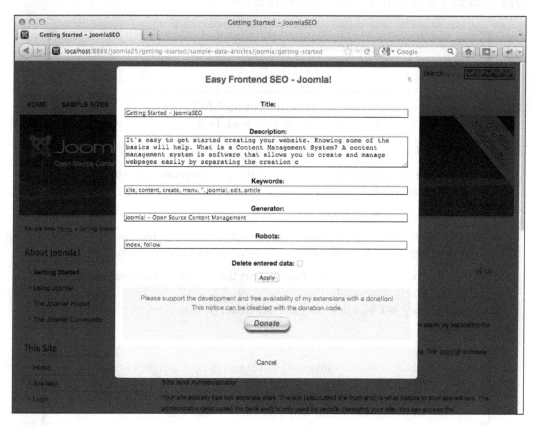

You can directly enter a title and the metadata for the page. Once finished, click on the **Apply** button and the window will close. As you view other pages, you can repeat the process.

# Setting up canonical URLs

For SEO purposes, you want to force all the URLs on your site to use a common structure. This is not only a best practices issue but also a way to reduce confusion and the possibility that your site may contain duplicate content (one article might appear both with and without the "www" prefix). The practice of standardizing the URL structure is known as creating canonical URLs.

 It doesn't really matter whether you use URLs with 'www' or without – the important thing is that it is consistent!

There are several ways you can set this up, but the SEO Canonicalization Plugin gives you a free and easy way to achieve this goal. Follow these steps:

1. Download and install the SEO Canonicalization Plugin, discussed earlier.
2. Access the **Plugin Manager** and find the plugin named **System – Canonicalization**. Click on it to open the editing screen for the plugin.
3. Change the **Status** to **Enabled**.
4. In the **Basic Options** column on the right-hand side, find the field labeled **Correct Host** and type the name of the domain you want your site to use.
5. Click on the **Check Settings** button and the system will attempt to verify that the domain is valid.
6. If everything is OK, click on **Save & Close**. (If not, correct the domain and try again!)

 There are some other options for this plugin, but they are not essential to the basic functionality. Move your mouse over the other options in the right-hand side column to view a description of what they do and why you might want to use them.

# Setting up your XML site map

XML site maps are an essential element of your SEO strategy. All the major search engines implement the XML site map standard, and you will certainly want to follow it on your site. The Xmap component, described earlier, gives you a simple way to implement this key functionality. Follow these steps to get started and create your first XML site map:

1. Download and install the Xmap extension, discussed earlier.

2. Visit the **Extension Manager**: Manage and find the component named **Xmap** and the plugin named **Xmap – Content Plugin**; enable both.

3. Select **Xmap** from the **Components** menu.

4. You will need to create your XML site map. To do this, click on the **New** icon on the top right-hand side. The New Sitemap page will open, as shown in the next screenshot.

5. Give the site map a **Title**: XML Site Map works just fine.

6. Set the **Status** to **Published**.

7. In the right-hand side **Menus** column, select the names of the menus whose items you wish to appear on the site map. Generally speaking, you will want to select all of them except the **Users** menu.

8. Click **Save & Close**.

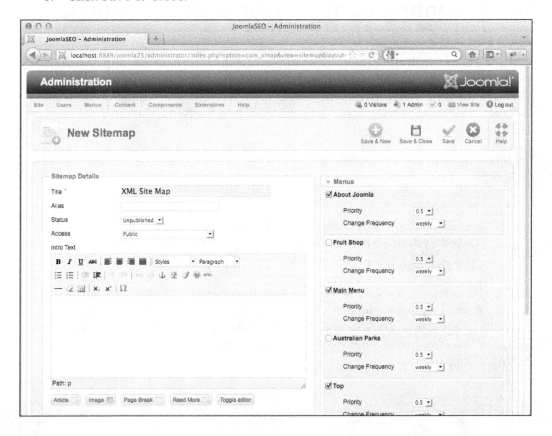

The site map is now active, but as discussed in the next chapter, you will need to submit the XML site map to the various registration services, particularly the Google and Bing Webmaster services.

 Note that you can also use this component to create site maps for your site visitors – simply make a new site map, link it to a menu, and style it as you like.

 The extension includes a number of plugins that help you with particular issues and third-party extensions. If you visit the Plug-in Manager, you will see that Xmap has given you tools to help with Kunena, SobiPro, and others. Enable only those that you need.

# Implementing control over your Alt and Title attributes

Alt and title attributes provide you with an additional chance to improve your key phrase density and also improve the accessibility of your content. You can add these elements manually, or you can add the SEO Friendly Links and Images extension to help generate them automatically. A combination of the two techniques offers your best coverage.

To implement the extension, follow these steps:

1. Download and install the SEO Friendly Links and Images extension, discussed earlier.
2. Access the **Plug-in Manager** from the **Extensions** menu. Find the option labeled **System – SEO Friendly Links and Images** and enable it.
3. Click the **Save & Close** icon.

The plugin is now active and will automatically add title attributes to links, and alt attributes to images. The default values will be generated from the link text or from the image name. You can override these default values at any time through the image or link insertion dialogues, or by manually inserting the values through the HTML editor.

# Setting up cross-posting to social networks

Providing site visitors with the ability to post links to your content on their social networks is a great way to encourage the creation of backlinks to your site. In the preceding section of this chapter, we highlighted several extensions that will enable social bookmarking and posting to various sites. One of those extensions, however, adds not only bookmarking to the most popular sites – Twitter, Facebook, and Google – but also taps into Facebook's comment functionality. Though not a complete social bookmarking solution, the Facebook-Twitter-Google+ extension is worth installing for the Facebook (and Twitter) integration it provides.

 Note that you will want to set up your Facebook and Twitter accounts first to get the most out of this extension. The **Advanced Options** tab, inside the plugins management screen, gives links to tutorials on how to set up these features.

To implement the plugin, follow these steps:

1. Download and install the Facebook-Twitter-Google+ extension, discussed earlier.

2. Access the **Plug-in Manager** from the **Extensions** menu. Find the option labeled **Content – Facebook – Twitter - Google+** and click on it to open the plugin's page, as shown in the next screenshot.

3. Select the choices you want from the **Basic Options** tab in the right-hand side column.

4. Click on the **Advanced Options** tab to access the additional features that allow for deeper integration with Facebook and Twitter, in particular.

5. Set the **Status** drop down to **Enabled**.

6. Click the **Save & Close** button.

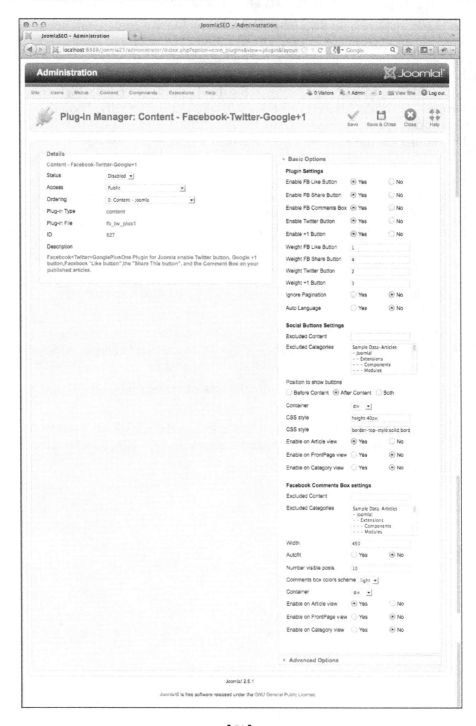

Once enabled, the plugin will display the choices you've selected on your content items, as seen in the next screenshot:

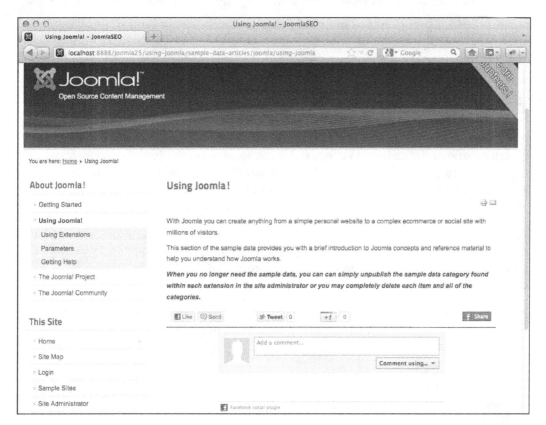

# Providing social bookmarking

While the Facebook-Twitter-Google+ extension, discussed in the previous section, allows users to post your articles to those sites, you may also want to install the Nice Social Bookmark extension, which adds coverage for a wider range of traditional social bookmarking sites, like Digg, Reddit, or StumbleUpon.

To set up the extension, follow these steps:

1. Download and install the Nice Social Bookmark extension.

2. Access the **Module Manager** from the **Extensions** menu. Find the option labeled **Nice Social Bookmark** and click on it to open the module's page.

3. Select the choices you want from the **Basic Options** tab in the right-hand side column.

4. Select the visibility options from the **Menu Assignment** section of the page.

5. Click on the **Select position** button and select where you want the icons to appear.

6. Change the **Status** dropdown to **Published**.

7. Click on the **Save & Close** icon.

# Summary

In this chapter we've looked at how you can add extensions to your site to enhance search engine optimization. We focused our attention on the Joomla! extensions directory, which contains a comprehensive listing of the options available for your site. Some of these extensions are simple and perform only one dedicated task, while others are more complex and offer a suite of tools rolled up into one single package.

This chapter identified the top SEO extensions for Joomla! 2.5.x and described what they can do for you. We covered both free and commercial extensions. We then showed you how you can install and configure a specific set of those extensions to create a solid foundation for your SEO efforts - all free of charge.

In the next chapter we will discuss what you need to do to get ready to launch your site; that is, the hands-on SEO work you should do in the lead up to launching (or re-launching) a site.

# 4
# Getting Ready for Launch

In previous chapters, we focused our discussion on the tools you need to get your site ready for an SEO campaign. This chapter focuses on the strategy side of things and looks at the decisions you need to make to create an effective SEO strategy for your site, how to implement that strategy, and how to get your site ready for launch.

The first portion of the chapter is focused on strategy, with an extensive discussion of approaches to keyword selection and a recommended process. Once you've decided on your strategy, you need to liaise with the content creators to assure that your search engine strategy is reflected in your content creation efforts. In the second part of the chapter we look at content strategies in detail. In the final portion of the chapter we look at some very useful third party tools that can assist you with getting your site into the search engines and thereafter assist with monitoring and tracking your efforts.

## Determining your SEO strategy

Do not underestimate the importance of creating a coherent SEO strategy. As we have stated several times in this book, SEO is a process. Like any process, you need to establish a set of parameters to guide the process, and help ensure that your efforts are coordinated and therefore more likely to help advance your overall goals. There are many factors that affect a site's search engine optimization, hence, no part of the process exists in isolation and it is necessary to make sure all your efforts keep the same goal in mind.

# Identifying keywords

For most companies, the initial steps in setting an SEO strategy focus on defining the product priorities and the target markets. As those issues are typically driven by the particular concerns of specific businesses, we're going to focus this discussion on the next step in the strategy process, that is, determining which keywords and phrases are most likely to deliver the type of traffic the site needs.

Start the keyword selection process by thinking big – don't restrict yourself by trying to formulate the most exact and narrow keyphrases; rather, come up with a large set of potentially relevant words and phrases that we can then whittle down to the optimal set. Look at the product or service; consider the language variants, the terms of art, and the related concepts. Make a list and add to it over time; this is one of those exercises that tends to benefit from having a bit of time to think about things and then process them. It's also a good idea to get other people involved to avoid subjective bias.

After you've assembled your preliminary list, it's best to take some time and do some research to make sure you haven't missed any candidate words or phrases. To accomplish this we'll use several techniques. One of the easiest ways to search for keyphrase ideas is to look at what is being done by your competitors. To do this, simply identify a set of competing sites, visit their sites, and then view the source code to see what, if anything, is in their metadata.

A useful tool for assisting with keyword selection is the Google AdWords Keyword Tool. It's free of charge and, despite the name, it's useful for a lot more than AdWords. Here's how to use it:

1. Direct your browser to `https://adwords.google.com/select/KeywordToolExternal.`

 Though you don't need to log in to Google to use the tool, you probably want to, as it unlocks additional functionality.

2. Open your list of potential keywords and copy the list.

3. Paste the list in the field marked **Word or phrase**. Put each word or phrase on a separate line.

4. Modify the **Advanced Options and Filters** to reflect the countries where your target markets reside and select the appropriate language and devices.

5. Complete the anti-Spam CAPTCHA field.

6. Click on the **Search** button.

The tool will then present you with a (potentially) long list of words and phrases that are related to your ideas, along with data about how frequently they were used by people searching on the Google search engine.

As an alternative to entering words or phrases as your starting point for keyword ideas, you can also point the tool to a particular web address. To use the website discovery tool, follow these steps:

1. Type the address of a competitor or other relevant website into the **Website** field.

2. Select the **Advanced Options and Filters**, as discussed earlier.

3. Complete the anti-Spam CAPTCHA field.

4. Click on the **Search** button.

Again, the tool presents you with a list of potential words and phrases, this time based on the content of a specific web page – a useful way to cross check your keyword ideas and discover new potential sources of traffic.

In addition to the list of words and phrases, the AdWords Keyword Tool also provides other useful information. The next screenshot shows a sample result set. The six words at the top, located under the heading **Search terms**, are the six words I entered into the **Word or phrase** field. The 800 words and phrases under the heading **Keyword ideas**, are those suggested by Google.

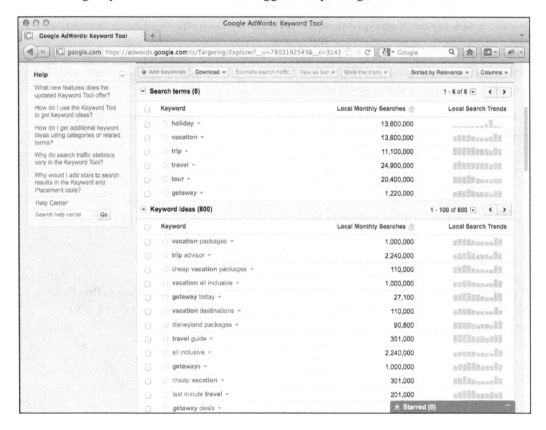

The two columns to the right-hand side of the keywords are important. The first, **Local Monthly Searches**, displays the number of times this keyword or phrase was entered into the Google search engine by a visitor; the number is a monthly average over the last 12 months. Click the combo box labeled **Sorted by Relevance** to change the sort criteria for the list of keywords, allowing you to easily spot the most popular keywords. You can now identify with confidence the keywords that are associated with the most traffic.

Using the **Columns** combo box, seen at the top right-hand side of the previous screenshot, you can select to view additional columns of data. One of the options allows you to display the average monthly traffic globally. This is a useful metric that allows you to compare global volume against the volume in the target markets you have selected.

The final column, **Local Search Trends,** contains 12 bars that display the relative search volume for the keyword in each of the last 12 months — a useful way of identifying trending terms.

### Targeting trends

If you are aggressively marketing products or services, you will want to try to take advantage of transient trends in search interest. As timeliness is the key, trend spotting for SEO purposes is best accomplished through research of real-time and near real-time services. Social media sites are often your best source of information about what's hot right now.

One of your best options for spotting trending topics is the Trends information provided to logged-in users by Twitter. While the default shows the top trending global topics, you can also filter the list by country and in some cases, by specific cities.

Another option is the Google Hot Trends page, which gives you a daily breakdown of the most popular searches. While the tool is free, it is very limited in that it only provides insights into broad search patterns and does not allow for granular or geographic filtering of the results. Explore Hot Trends at http://www.google.com/trends/hottrends.

Another tool from Google is called Google Insights for Search (http://www.google.com/insights/search/). While this tool is not terribly convenient for discovering trending terms, it is useful for validating and quantifying trends. It also allows for filtering by date and location, which can be used to fine tune your targeting.

Now that you have a set of key words that have a known ability to deliver traffic, you need to select which ones to target for your efforts. You're not going to be able to target all the relevant, or even necessarily the most desirable, keyphrases. For most people, this comes down to a cost/benefit analysis. Be selective and pick a limited set that represents the best choices for your site.

If you are like most people, at this point you will want to get your keywords data out of the Google Keyword Tool and into a tool that allows you to manipulate the data more easily. Google makes this easy to do; simply click the checkbox next to the words you want to keep then click the **Download** button and select the format for the file. You will then be able to open the keyword list and manipulate it in Excel, or your preferred spreadsheet program. If you don't see the **Download** option, log in to Google.

Note that the Google AdWords External Keyword Tool is only one tool for identifying potential keywords for your site. While the Google tool enjoys the benefit of being free of charge, if you are out to be more competitive and dig more deeply into keyphrase research, you will want to explore commercial offerings such as SEMRush (http://www.semrush.com), Trellian KW Discovery tool (http://www.keyworddiscovery.com/), WordStream (http://www.wordstream.com/keywords), or WordTracker (http://www.wordtracker.com/). Another useful free tool is Ubersuggest (http://ubersuggest.org/).

The decision of which keyphrases are the best choice for any particular site is a subjective one. If you are concerned about fast results or responding to seasonal demand patterns, you will be looking at trending keyphrases and those with high volume. If you are looking at long term brand building or product awareness, you may be selecting words that most accurately describe your products or services, regardless of whether those terms generate less traffic than other less specific keywords.

**How many keywords?**

How many keyword or phrases should you target? The answer is: It depends. Generally, a large site with significant content has more opportunities for traffic acquisition via keyword optimization. It's simple math: The more content (and the broader the content), the more potentially relevant keywords. A good rule of thumb is to not attempt to target more than two or three keyphrases for any single URL.

You can be certain that you are not the only person who has determined that a particular keyphrase is valuable. There will always be competition. While you can blindly pursue the highest volume keyphrases without consideration of the competition for those phrases, we cannot recommend that approach; it is a recipe for slow, or no, results. If you wish to target high traffic and high competition keywords, be prepared for a long fight for ranking (and thereafter an on-going struggle to maintain those rankings). The low-hanging fruit is in the long tail, that is, the keyphrases found near the narrow end of the search query frequency or competition distribution.

Chasing the long tail has several advantages:

- Competition tends to be lower, thereby increasing your chances of ranking well
- Conversion rates tend to be higher, typically because there is a correlation between the length (or specificity, if you prefer) of the keyphrase and its position on the tail, that is, the longer the keyphrase, the further it is towards the end of the tail

[  The long tail is typically populated by longer, more specific keyphrases. ]

Reaping the rewards of a long tail is much easier than competing against large numbers of sites for broad key words. While there are literally millions of sites competing for the phrase "caribbean villa", there are significantly fewer chasing the phrase "2 bedroom villa rental in Curacao". Moreover, if someone is looking specifically to rent a "2 bedroom villa in Curacao", and you have one available on your site, then this is just the sort of visitor you want. In contrast, if someone is simply searching for "caribbean villa", you have no idea what island is of interest, or even whether they want to rent or buy – in other words, they may not be the customers you are looking for.

# Assessing keyword effectiveness

While keyphrase selection is more an art than a science, there are metrics you can apply to the process. One of the most useful is known as the **Keyword Effectiveness Index**, or **KEI**.

KEI, in its simplest form, is a comparison of the potential search volume for a term relative to the number of pages competing for that term. There are multiple methodologies for arriving at KEI; which approach you prefer will typically depend on your personal SEO strategy. The most direct KEI formula looks as follows:

$$KEI = V^2/C$$

Where:

- $V$ = Volume of search queries for the term
- $C$ = number of pages competing for the term

In other words, KEI is the square of the search query volume divided by the number of competing pages.

> Why do we take the square of the volume figure? This is done in order to take into account the popularity of the query. Without the multiplier, a term that averages only two queries a month, but has 100 competitors, would get the same KEI as a term that averages 200 queries a month and has 10,000 competitors. This is anomalous, as clearly the term with 200 queries a month is more desirable. By introducing a multiplier to the equation, we reward more popular queries with a higher KEI.

Let's put the formula into practice: If you look at the Google Keyword Tool screenshot earlier in this chapter, you can see that the search term **last minute travel** generated an average of **201,000** queries per month over the last year; that's the first piece of data we need. Now, we need to find the number of pages competing. To do that, simply go to Google and run a search for **last minute travel**. At the top of the search results, Google tells you how many results were found, as seen in the following screenshot:

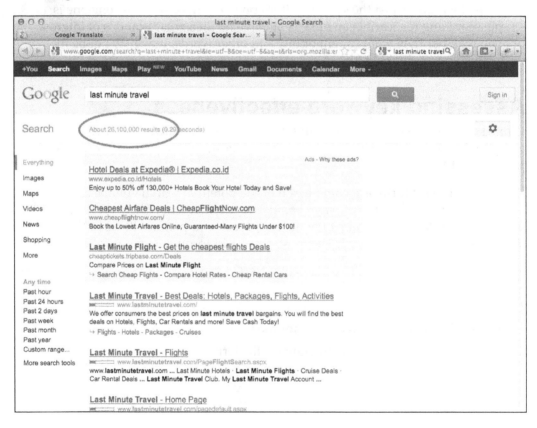

Now we have both of the numbers we need:

$$201,000^2/26,100,000 = 1547.9$$

Accordingly, using this measure of keyword effectiveness, we can say that the phrase **last minute travel** has a KEI of 1547.9. We could then run the rest of our candidate keyphrases through the same exercise and create an objective benchmark that could be used to compare the relative attractiveness of each of the various words and phrases.

In the example given, we looked to Google.com for data. Depending on your target markets, you may well want to check instead the country-specific versions of Google. Note that your choice of geographic filters in the Google Keyword Tool should be consistent with your selection of the appropriate Google search engine. In the example given, the Keyword Tool was set to produce results relevant to the United States, and the competition data was then taken from Google.com, as it is by far the most popular choice for web searches in the U.S.; you should apply a similar logic if you are targeting non-U.S., or non-English-speaking markets.

As noted previously, there are multiple approaches to calculating KEI. One alternative addresses (at least in part) the most common criticism of KEI, that is, that KEI does not take into account the quality of the competition. Use this variation on the KEI formula to restrict your competition analysis to only the more aggressive competitors. To narrow the analysis to a more accurate list of serious competitors, search only for those pages that use the keyphrase in the page titles, rather than using the gross search results figure from Google. To do this, we modify our search query for competing pages. Instead of searching for all mentions of the phrase, we can use the Google search operator **allintitle**. Your modified search query to Google will look like this: **allintitle: last minute travel**. With this operator in the query, you will get a count of only those pages where the term **last minute travel** is included in the page title – a reasonably effective way of narrowing things down to the number of sites that are making a serious effort to compete for traffic from the keyphrase. In the example used here, the competition number drops from over 26 million to 767,000.

Another useful variation on the KEI formula is to factor in a relevance rating for each keyphrase. To do this, you must first rate all the prospective keyphrases for relevance. This is a subjective exercise, so any criteria you use is fine, as long as it is logically consistent. The easiest solution is to simply rate each keyword on a scale of 1 to 3, where 1 is the least relevant, and 3 is the most relevant. To apply, modify the formula as follows:

$$KEI = (V^2/C)R$$

Where:

- V = Volume of search queries for the term
- C = number of pages competing for the term
- R = your relevance ranking

In other words, take the square of the search query volume, divide it by the number of competing pages, and then finally multiple the result by the relevance ranking.

Of course, you can always combine both of these variations, or you can create your own version of this popular formula. Regardless of which path you choose, using an objective metric to assess the possible keyphrases is a useful exercise. Not only does it allow you to impose a transparent methodology to assessing keywords, but also helps decision makers formulate an appropriate cost/benefit analysis for chasing particular keyphrases.

 One final point – and it should go without saying — never forget that the suitability of content is always an issue. It does you no good to blindly select keywords based solely on search volume; to see success, the phrases must be relevant to the content on the URL you are targeting.

# Tapping into the power of stemming and variants

The major search engines are, to varying degrees, capable of identifying similar and related words. If you are aware of this, you can use it to your advantage in both your keyphrase selection strategy and in your content creation. Two techniques are of primary use here: stemming and word variants.

Stemming is simply reducing a word to its root form. To take a simple example, the word "take" has multiple acceptable forms: take, taken, taking, took. Other words have irregular plural forms, for example, "child" and "children." Most search engines will recognize the various grammatical forms and derivations and return them when a user searches for the root word, though they will not be given the same relevance as the root.

In terms of keyword strategy, this presents an opportunity. Your search for the optimal keywords should also look at the word roots that are relevant to your site and compare the traffic for the roots and the other forms. Based on the results, you can then decide whether to target the root, or a specific derivation. Stemming also gives webmasters more latitude when writing content, empowering the use of alternative forms that are closely related. By varying your word choice in your content, you can avoid boring repetitions that alienate readers and keyword stuffing that alienates search engines.

Variants, in this context, refers to the use of synonyms, alternative spellings, and common misspellings. As with stemming, you should always investigate the options presented by variants in your assessment of the optimal keyphrases. Synonym usage, in particular, can often provide very fertile ground. Differences in British and American English is also an area that should be investigated, particularly where your target markets use mixed (some spell it one way, others another) spellings. Misspellings can also provide some pleasant surprises, opening up low competition avenues to search engine traffic.

**Does capitalization matter?**

Yes, it does. Traditionally in search, if a user enters a query in lower case, the engine will return all results, both upper and lower case. If the user entered upper case (capitalized text), the search engine would only return upper case results. The logic for this was simple: Words entirely in capitals are most likely acronyms, with distinct or specialized meanings. Words in title case (that is, first letter only capitalized), most likely refer to proper names, including places or brands.

While Google and other major search engines exhibit much more flexibility and no longer implement the rule strictly (at least in basic search), your use of capitalization should reflect accurately the content. If you are dealing with a person, place, or brand, use title case. If you are dealing with an acronym, use ALL CAPS. For everything else, use lower case.

# Content strategies for enhancing search engine ranking

The old cliché "content is king" managed to become both old and a cliché by benefitting from an additional attribute: accuracy. The search engines themselves, despite being notoriously reluctant to share insights into their priorities, have consistently made it clear that they consider the content of your site the most influential attribute in keyphrase relevance and ranking. It's no joke: When it comes to SEO, content is the undisputed king.

The issue of the importance of content has multiple facets; don't make the mistake of thinking that it is enough to simply have large amounts of content. There are three aspects of content that greatly affect the amount of influence it has on a site's ranking: relevancy, recency, and quantity.

Relevancy is the top priority. If you want to rank well for the phrase "vintage mustang parts", then your page had better contain information about vintage mustang parts. A single mention of the keyphrase on the page isn't going to do the job either; the content needs to discuss the topic in some detail to get the maximum benefit from the presence of related words and phrases. The search engines look for context clues that help them dial in the relevance for a page, hence they determine meaning not from simple phrases or sentences, but from entire blocks of text (this is sometimes referred to as "block analysis").

The concept of keyword density is worth mentioning here. The phrase refers to the percentage of times that a keyword or phrase appears on a page. The theory is that with too many keywords on the page you will risk being penalized for keyword stuffing; too few and your relevance ranking suffers. Calculating a page's keyword density is simple: count the number of times a particular word or phrase is mentioned on the page, then divide by the total number of words on the page. However, this topic is not without controversy. Some SEO experts consider optimum density to be in the range of .002 to .004. Others say it just doesn't matter, and that keyword density is a stale concept. From our perspective, obsessing on keyword density is probably not the best use of your time. Today's search engines seem to attach less importance to frequency and rather more weight to the occurrence of terms in the top portion of the content item, in the headings, and of course, in the page title and URL. Work on creating natural, readable text and be concerned more with the prominence and position of the keywords on the page, than with the density. There is one thing everyone agrees on, however: Don't keyword stuff!

Another factor to consider is the recency and frequency of change of your content. While this is more of an issue for on-going site maintenance, it's relevant to the discussion here. It is widely believed that the search engines not only assess how recently the page was updated, but also the frequency with which the content on the site changes, and how that update rate changes from period to period. Accordingly, an on-going challenge for your webmaster is the creation of new pages and the updating of stale ones. As new pages are created, make sure you add internal links to and/or from older pages, both to improve link density and to encourage people to explore your site further.

The concept is pretty straightforward, but to put it into an easy-to-use list, here are the important points:

- Create new content. Adding new pages at a higher rate than your competitors gives an advantage.
- Update old content regularly.
- The larger the extent of an update to a page, the better.
- The frequency of change is a factor; more frequent changes are better.
- Changes to content above the fold are more important than changes in less important areas of the page.

The final factor to discuss here is quantity, and this is by far the simplest point. In short, more is better! All things being equal, a site with more relevant content enjoys an advantage over its competitors. Note this important caveat: When we talk here about content, we mean quality, original content. Merely reproducing articles that appear elsewhere on the web is not a valid content strategy for boosting your site's rankings. Similarly, creating tons of low quality or repetitious content won't help you either; indeed, it's more likely to hurt you.

**The importance of a concerted effort**

While you should be concerned about the quality of your content, do not lose sight of the fact that a highly effective site is the result of a number of factors working in concert. Not only do you need to be concerned about the technical issues discussed in the previous chapters, but you also need to make sure that all your efforts are made in light of your overall strategy and are consistent in their emphasis of your target concepts.

When it comes to creating content, don't neglect the other elements on that page, as some of those are significant influencers on perceptions of relevance, as discussed in the following:

- The article's title is key. It should employ the keyphrase and it should be formatted with an appropriate H tag (probably H2).
- Similarly, any sub-heading in the article should try to employ the keyphrase or variants and should employ H tags (probably H3, H4, H5, and so on).
- The page's URL is also key and should reflect the keyphrase.
- Links pointing to the page (internal or inbound) should employ relevant link text and should use the title attribute.
- Images on the page should have captions and alt attribute text that reinforces the keyphrase or related concept. (The name of the image file itself is also useful, particularly for ranking in Google Image Search.)
- The metadata for the page should be consistent with the page content and reinforce key concepts, picking up variants and stems.
- Post links back to the content on social media sites when you publish it.
- Make sure you update your XML site map to include new content items.

 In the discussion above, what happened to the H1 tag? Simple. Best practice is to use that tag for your site name and/or tagline.

# Setting up third party services that can assist with SEO

Once your site is built and populated with content, but prior to launching for the general public, you will want to take some preliminary steps to get the site ready for the search engines. In this section of the chapter we highlight three helpful third party tools you should put in place for launch:

- Google Analytics
- Google Webmaster Tools
- Bing Webmaster Tools

All three tools require you to have accounts on the various services (that is, Google and Bing). In this text, we'll assume you have already registered for accounts on Google and Bing and will be using those accounts to get things set up for your site.

Note, that if you are setting up a site that you intend to hand off to a client, you will probably want to create a unique account for them, or use one of the client's existing accounts. Transferring ownership of accounts is problematic and best avoided.

# Getting started with Google Analytics

Google Analytics is a website traffic tracking program. The tool is free of charge, loaded with features, and an excellent choice for most website owners. If you are not familiar with the service, you should take some time to explore the tutorials Google offers, as fluency with the tool can be of great benefit to your SEO efforts. With Google Analytics on your site, you can track site visitor activity and discover where they came from, how long they spent on the site, and what they looked at on your site. The system also tracks inbound search traffic and provides you with invaluable feedback on which keywords are generating traffic for your site in which markets.

You can learn more at http://www.google.com/analytics/ where you can create an account and explore a number of help resources from Google.

Implementing the service takes three steps:

1. Create a Google Analytics account for the domain.
2. Copy the tracking code provided by Google Analytics and add it to the pages of the site.
3. Verify the site.

If you are working on a site rebuild, we advise against creating a new Google Analytics account. The better option is generally to use the existing site's Analytics code, which thereby preserves the site's traffic history and allows you to benchmark against historical data after you launch the new site.

In Joomla! there are several extensions that allow you to avoid having to copy and paste code – you need to only add the Google I.D. to the extension and it will handle getting the code into the right place on each of the pages. If you are not using one of the extensions that includes Google Analytics management, you will need to edit the files of your Joomla! template to add the code in the right place on the page. While it's hard to go wrong here, you should note the placement of the code: It belongs just before the closing </head> tag. If there are other scripts in the <head> section of your page, put them before the Google Analytics tracking code.

Most Joomla! templates use a shared `index.php` file that contains the <head> for all the pages on your site. If that is the case with your template, then you need to only paste the tracking code one time (that is, just before the closing </head> tag in the `index.php` file inside your active template folder).

Once the code is inserted into your template file, save it, then check it by viewing the site in your browser and then viewing the page source. If you don't see the Google Analytics tracking code, go back and check your work and try again.

 Note that verifying the site can only be done if the site is online.

# Working with Google Webmaster Tools

Google Webmaster Tools is a free service provided by Google to help site owners gain insights into their web pages' visibility on Google. The service allows you to gain information about when and how deeply the site was spidered and whether there were any errors found. From a pure SEO perspective, the service is also quite useful as it allows you to identify search query traffic and maintain a count of inbound links. Additionally, the service provides a place for you to register your XML site map, and monitor whether it is functioning properly.

 Visit Google Webmaster Tools at `https://www.google.com/webmasters/tools`.

To get started with Google Webmaster Tools, you need to create an account and then verify the ownership of your site. The system provides you with alternative ways to verify your account, but for most people the easiest way will typically be to download the HTML file Google provides and then move it up to the root of the domain you are registering.

Once you have verified the domain, you should take two further steps. First, let's connect our two Google accounts and let the Webmaster Tools service share information with the Analytics service. Once you link the accounts, you'll be able to see Webmaster Tools data in your Google Analytics reports and you'll also be able to access Analytics report data directly from relevant pages inside Google Webmaster Tools.

To link the accounts, follow these steps:

1. Log in to Google Webmaster Tools.

2. On the Webmaster Tools home page click on the **Manage Site** link (next to the name of the site you want to link) and select the option **Google Analytics property**.

3. On the page that loads, select the radio button next to the Analytics property you want to associate with the site.

4. Click on the **Save** button.

The next step to take after you have verified your account is to notify Google about the existence of your XML site map. To add your site map, follow these steps:

1. Log in to Google Webmaster.

2. On the Webmaster Tools home page, click on the name of your site to open the site management page.

3. Select the option **Sitemaps**, under Site configuration.

4. On the page that loads, click the **Add/Test Sitemap** button on the top right-hand side of the page.

5. In the pop-up that appears, enter the URL of your XML site map.

6. Click on the **Submit Sitemap** button.

That's all there is to it. Google will put the URL for your sitemap in the queue to be spidered and once it is spidered, the results will be viewable inside the Google Webmaster Tools system; if there were errors, they will also be shown.

 You will want to check back in a day or so to make sure your sitemap has been indexed properly, and if not, troubleshoot it.

In addition to its ability to help you track keyword traffic and inbound links, Google Webmaster Tools provides a set of useful diagnostic tools to help you keep your site fine tuned. You will want to check into your account periodically to check for error reports, and to look at how your site is being spidered. It's a good idea to monitor the depth of the spidering and to make sure that all your pages are being indexed.

The system contains additional tips to help you with issues like your `robots.txt` file, possible malware infestations, and canonical URL settings.

> One of the more interesting tools is the option to view your site as Google sees it. This allows you to check your site's code by looking at it in the same fashion that it is seen by Google's indexing spider, the Googlebot. It's a simple way to make sure your most critical information is clearly visible to the spider and not buried under tons of irrelevant code, scripts, and other noise. To use this tool, select the options **View site as Googlebot**.

# Working with Bing Webmaster Tools

Bing Webmaster Tools is, essentially, a parallel service to Google Webmaster Tools. The service is provided free of charge by Bing and allows you to perform the same basic tasks you can find on Google Webmaster Tools. Indeed, there are more similarities between the services than differences; the key difference being that Bing Webmaster Tools provides data for both Bing and Yahoo!.

> Visit Bing Webmaster Tools at `http://www.bing.com/toolbox/webmaster/`.

To set up Bing Webmaster Tools for your site, simply create an account for the domain and then verify your ownership of the site. The system provides several alternatives for verifying your ownership of the domain; the easiest is probably to upload the XML file that Bing provides during the setup process.

After your site is verified, it's time to add your XML site map. Follow these steps:

1. Log in to Bing Webmaster Tools.
2. Click on the name of your site.
3. On the page that loads, click on the **Crawl** tab at the top of the page.
4. On the **Crawl Summary** page, click on the **Sitemaps (XML, Atom, RSS)** link, either at the top, under the tabs, or in the left-hand side navigation column.
5. On the **Sitemaps** page, click on the **Add Feed** button.
6. Type the URL of your XML site map in the pop-up that appears.
7. Click on the **Submit** button.

Your XML is now queued to be crawled by the Bing spider; check back in a day or so to verify that it was successful and free from errors.

# Summary

This chapter was the first to look at the soft factors – the strategy side of SEO. The key point is that it is necessary to engage in planning to create a relevant and practical SEO strategy for your site before you start your work, and to then implement that strategy in a consistent and structured fashion. In this chapter, we looked at techniques for selecting key words and phrases, with an emphasis on using the Keyword Effectiveness Index (KEI).

Once you have a solid strategy and a set of keywords, it's time to get to work. In this chapter, we looked at how content creation relates to SEO and discussed the three factors that webmasters should keep in mind: relevance, recency, and quantity.

Prior to launch, you should also put in place several tools that will help you monitor and maintain your site. We looked at what they do and how to get started with each of them. The three systems serve varying purposes. Google Analytics is a powerful web traffic reporting tool that lets you monitor your site traffic and inbound keyphrase performance. Google Webmaster and Bing Webmaster provide a set of useful tools focused on assessing how the site is being indexed by the search engines and provide you with a way to monitor indexing and keep your XML site maps up to date.

At the end of this chapter, you should have a site that is ready for launch. In previous chapters we covered the technical foundations. In this chapter we talked about strategy and implementation. In the final chapter in this text, we look at on-going maintenance and enhancement of your SEO efforts.

# 5
# Managing SEO on a Live Site

As we discussed in *Chapter 1, An Introduction to Search Engine Optimization*, SEO is not something you can do once and then forget about. This chapter looks at the steps you should take to help enhance and maintain your ranking once the site has gone live, as well as how to track and assess the success of your efforts.

Topics covered in this chapter include link building, social media optimization, and how to track and measure your SEO performance over time.

## Link building

Link building should be part of your on-going efforts to generate traffic and improve your site's organic search ranking. Looking at link building in the context of SEO, your best bet for success lies in emphasizing growth in the number of quality links that point to your site. In short, the more high quality links you have pointing to your site, the better. The search engines' view on this point is simple: If your content is authoritative and valuable, other people will link to it. If the people linking to your content are also viewed as being authoritative, then the search engines consider the value of their links to be greater than links from a low authority website.

While links have traditionally been important influencers on relevancy ranking, it's important to understand that not all links are equal, at least not in the eyes of the search engines. Recent changes in the Google algorithm have been aimed at rooting out artificial link building strategies and minimizing their ability to impact rank. From a best practices perspective, link building (or "link marketing" if you prefer) should not be viewed primarily as an exercise in manipulating rank, but rather as a means of increasing your site's influence and reach. Don't obsess on building the greatest number of links; rather, focus on building strategic links and exposing your high quality content to the widest range of people.

**Watch out for nofollow!**

`nofollow` is a value available to the link relation attribute of the HTML `link` or a elements. At the code level, the attribute looks as follows:

```
<a href="http://hyperlink.com" rel="nofollow">Link
text</a>
```

When the `nofollow` value is specified in the `rel` attribute, search engines will not follow and index the link. In the event that `nofollow` is not specified, the search engine spiders will follow the link (assuming that the spiders have not been blocked from indexing in some other fashion).

In the context of link building, this is a crucial issue. Adding your link to a site that specifies `nofollow` on links means that you gain no SEO benefit from the existence of the link. Before you add your link to a site, it is essential that you examine the site's source code to make sure that the outbound links are not using `nofollow`.

Links fall into three broad categories:

- **Organic links**: These are links to your site that are voluntarily given by others. Organic links are normally a by-product of excellent content that people want to share.

- **Solicited links**: Links obtained by reaching out to another site and requesting a link. This would include links you purchase, reciprocal links, and other similar schemes.

- **Self-created links**: Links that you create by posting content on other sites. This category includes article submissions, press releases, forum posts, comments, and proactive social sharing.

Of the three, self-created links are the easiest to obtain, as the act of link creation is completely within your control. The first two categories require effort over time and are really outside your control; whether you get the link is not up to you (unless, of course, you're buying the link). In the sections coming up next, we look at how to identify potential link partners and how to structure a link building campaign.

*Never lose site of the fact that ranking well is merely a means to an end. For most site owners, the ultimate goal of engaging in an SEO campaign is the creation of relevant referral traffic, be it from search engines or from other sites. Links can be instrumental in driving qualified traffic and should be viewed primarily from this perspective.*

# Identifying quality link partners

The process of finding quality link partners begins with a search for relevant sites. The goal is to identify sites that will return the highest value in exchange for the amount of effort you have to invest. Once you have identified candidates, you must look at the value those links will generate and rank them as priorities for your efforts.

How do you find potential link partners? There are multiple techniques you can apply, but often the easiest is to first look to your competitors and identify the sites that have given them inbound links; the rationale is that if another site was interested in your competitors, they might very well be interested in you. While there are tools that will help you spot inbound links to competitor sites, you can accomplish a lot on your own by simply going to Google and running a search on the competitor's domain name using the query parameter **link:**.

 To find all the pages linking to the site packtpub.com, for example, you would enter this query into the Google search field: **link:packtpub.com**.

Once you have a list of all your competitors' inbound links, you can set out to chase them down and request links to your content. Following the path laid down by your competitors is, however, the low-hanging fruit. You will most certainly want to do more.

If you don't have the time to manually search for your competitors' link partners, or you need to search a large number of domains, try using Open Site Explorer (`http://opensiteexplorer.org`). Simply enter the URL of your competitor's site and the system will return a list of all links related to that site. Filter the list to show only external links, and then export the data as a `.csv` file. Import that `.csv` file into your favorite spreadsheet program and you have a list of your competitor's links, ready for you to contact.

 Note that while you can use Open Site Explorer free of charge, you do have to be a subscriber to use the `.csv` file download feature. Registration also unlocks more features.

If you want to go one step further, take the `.csv` file from Open Site Explorer and import it to LinkDetective (`http://www.linkdetective.com`). LinkDetective is a free service that leverages the data from Open Site Explorer. Using the tool, you can obtain in-depth information about your competitors' links and know which are the most attractive for you to target.

Following the paths trodden by your competitors is only one way to discover potential link partners. Google and Bing are two of your most valuable tools, allowing you to track down relevant sites by using a variety of search techniques. Running a simple search on your keywords is one way to find relevant sites with high rankings, but you may want to consider using several of Google's search parameters to refine your hunt:

- Use **allintitle: keyword(s)** to find pages where your keywords appear in the page title

- Use **allinurl: keyword(s)** to restrict the search results to only those pages where the keywords are part of the URL

- Use **allinanchor: keyword(s)** to find links where the keywords appear in the anchor text for links

- Use **allintext: keyword(s)** to find pages that have the highest relevance for your keywords in the content of the page

Similar tools for some of these options exist on Bing and on other major search engines.

> The process of discovering link partners requires creative thinking and research ability. While using search parameters (like those outlined previously) provide a good starting point, you will want to dive much deeper to find the best opportunities. BuzzStream provides a free Link Building Query Generator that can save you quite a bit of time. Simply enter information about your brand, your competitors, and your market, and the tool will generate a number of potentially useful queries for both Google and Bing. This tool is a great way to kick start your link prospecting. To try out the tool, visit http:// tools.buzzstream.com/link-building-query-generator.

Once you have your list of potential link prospects, the next step is to assess which can deliver the most value to you. Not all links are of equal importance. As stated earlier, your emphasis should be on building quality links to your site, and quality links come from high value and authoritative sites. There are several useful metrics that can help you identify the most attractive link prospects. Among the best and most widely-used metrics are the following:

- Alexa Rank: http://alexa.com

- MozRank and MozTrust: http://opensiteexplorer.org

- Google PageRank: Use the Google Toolbar (for Internet Explorer only, unfortunately) or install the SEOQuake toolbar (http://seoquake.com) for your favorite browser

It should go without saying, but to be an effective link partner (for SEO relevancy purposes) the site should be relevant and authoritative for the content on your site. If your site is about colonial furniture, for example, getting links from a site about fly fishing won't be much help to you, even if the fly fishing site is highly rated, as it is not authoritative on the subject of furniture.

# Managing a link marketing campaign

Link building is undoubtedly the most tedious and frustrating part of any SEO campaign. Though automation programs exist, they are of extremely little use in obtaining quality links. Automated link submission systems are really intended to get you large numbers of links, not help you identify and approach authoritative sites. The systems typically target online directories and other sites that gather links and organize them topically. Few of those sites, however, provide you with quality inbound links. Many of them exist for no other purpose than for creating links and their indexes are filled with low quality, spammy websites. If you have a quality site, you don't want to be there and you should avoid them.

The most reliable approach for building high quality links is also the most traditional, that is, creating a relationship with a site's publisher. Direct e-mails to a site owner, or to authors on a site, are a great way to expand your network and introduce your content to influencers. Seek out other avenues of outreach as well. If the site offers a contact form, use that to introduce yourself to the site owner. Don't forget about the telephone – a phone call can sometimes produce results faster than any other means of contact.

Every site publisher is used to seeing their inbox fill up with form e-mails from people asking for links. It's a huge turnoff to receive form e-mails that show no attempt at personalization, no attempt to explain why creating a relationship is useful or appropriate, or even worse, horrid grammar and spelling. Publishers will – rightfully – throw those messages straight into the trash (or mark them as junk!). Effective outreach involves the personal touch and shows a clear effort to demonstrate value and relevance that would motivate a publisher to engage in a dialogue.

Your link building efforts will eat up a fair amount of time and will require follow up. Given that there are often delays in response times, it's important that you impose some structure on your efforts, else you tend to lose track of things and your effectiveness is diluted. While there are software tools to help with link discovery and with tracking your contacts and link requests, often the simplest tool is the best: Create a spreadsheet, set up columns for the site name, URL, contact person, contact address, and contact history. Use the spreadsheet to log your efforts and create a schedule for follow up. It's a cheap, simple, and effective way to impose order on a link building campaign.

If you have the budget and the inclination to use a commercial tool for researching and managing your link building campaign, one of the more attractive options is Ontolo. This system is available on a monthly subscription basis and gives you access to their link discovery and campaign management dashboard. Ontolo includes a number of useful tools, including very good competitor analysis and tracking. To learn more, visit `http://ontolo.com`.

Another option, with more flexible pricing, is Buzzstream. Like Ontolo, BuzzStream helps you discover potential link partners and manage your campaigns. The system also keeps track of backlinks and helps you monitor the status of your links. To learn more, visit `http://buzzstream.com`.

Content creation also has an important role in link marketing. If you are able to inspire others to link to your site solely on the strength of your content, then you will be well ahead in the game. Moreover, one-way links given freely, based on editorial content are effective ways to generate traffic. The content can take many forms. Some of the best proven approaches for creating interesting content include:

- Top ten lists
- "Best of" lists
- Humor, including funny videos
- Infographics
- Great photos
- Controversial articles
- "How to" and tutorials

Creating content items designed to generate links is sometimes referred to as creating "link bait".

# Creating your own links

There are literally tens of thousands of sites on the web that present opportunities for you to create your own links. These opportunities take a variety of forms:

- Directories
- Comments
- Forum posts
- Content aggregators
- "Submit your site" opportunities
- Press release distribution
- Article exchanges
- Video sharing sites
- Document sharing sites

Use these options to create a varied collection of inbound links and to raise the profile of your site. Don't waste these opportunities by posting spammy comments or blatant plugs; rather use them to establish your site as a relevant authority and source of useful information. Directly plugging your site, particularly in comments or forums, will earn nothing but deletion or a ban on your IP.

When embedding links back to your site, make an effort to write good anchor text. Your choice of anchor text should help reinforce your keyword strategy, but more importantly, it should be natural and should represent the actual content of the destination page. Google has given indications that it is sensitive to unnatural anchor text. Too many repetitions of the same phrase may, in fact, signal to Google that the links are artificial and therefore de-value them.

When a search engine indexes a link, the anchor text in that link is viewed as an indicator of what the destination page is about. Using the fly fishing example again, a solid application of link text might be "fly fishing for trout in montana" in contrast to "fly fishing, fishing gear, fishing tips, montana fly fishing" – the latter example would be more likely to be considered unnatural and indicative of an attempt to manipulate the page's relevancy ranking.

# Directories

One of the easiest ways to get links is to submit your site to some of the many directories on the web. Listing in major directories, such as the Yahoo! Directory (`http://dir.yahoo.com`) or Business.com (`http://www.business.com`), offers some benefit, but almost all of the quality directories with a broad content focus require a listing fee. If you have the budget, you may want to consider some of these broad (non-specialized) directories, as listing is assured upon payment of the fee.

[  The largest free directory, DMOZ (`http://dmoz.org`) is extremely slow to accept new sites and is largely an exercise in frustration. ]

Some of the best directories out there are, however, niche directories. These topical directories focus on a specific topic and are often viewed as a relevant authority in their field. If your site is similar in topic, niche directories can provide worthwhile inbound links. Moreover, from a traffic generation point of view, topical directories can be good sources of quality traffic, regardless of whether they are significantly persuasive to your site's search engine ranking.

Though not technically, directories don't overlook sites that provide for their visitors lists of relevant resources. These "mini-directories" are typically topical and often worth the effort of seeking out for their link value.

[

**Identifying quality directories**

Despite the proliferation of low-quality web directories, there are a few winners out there. How do you identify a quality directory?

 Page ranking indicators are useful, but don't just look at the home page. You should always look at the rank of the page where your link will appear. Often you will find that while the directory's home page has a solid ranking, the page where your link will appear has a much less desirable rank; if that's the case, think carefully about how much value this will deliver to you.

Finally, trust your instincts. How does the directory look to you? Is the appearance high quality? Is it current? Is it filled with spammy websites? Would you trust it for a site recommendation? If it looks dodgy and feels dodgy, it probably is dodgy – avoid it.

]

# Press releases

Press releases, video sharing, and file sharing deserve special mention. While the creation of the content to feed these services is time consuming, the rewards can be significant. There are a number of useful free press release distribution services, including:

- Free Press Release (http://free-press-release.com)
- i-Newswire (http://i-newswire.com)
- PRinside (http://pr-inside.com)
- PRLog (http://prlog.org)

Posting your press release on those sites will get the releases indexed quickly. Moreover, some offer premium plans that add social bookmarking and other advanced indexing features. In addition to the free services, there are several very good commercial services worth considering, including PRWeb (http://www.prweb.com), PRLeap (http://www.prleap.com), and WebWire (http://www.webwire.com). These services offer expedited listings, expanded distribution, and options for adding supplementary media.

 When you set up your press release, make sure you use the contact information section to add links and descriptive text.

# Video and file sharing

Video and file sharing sites can be excellent sources of traffic. While YouTube is the big brand in the video world, don't forget about the large number of additional sites for distributing your video content, in particular:

- DailyMotion (http://dailymotion.com)
- MetaCafe (http://metacafe.com)
- PhotoBucket (http://photobucket.com)
- Veoh (http://veoh.com)
- Vimeo (http://vimeo.com)

Photo sharing offers another option to create traffic and, in some cases, links. Use the photos as a resource for your other efforts, as well, linking to the image in social bookmarking sites, social media, and blog posts. The description field for the image also gives you a place to add descriptive copy.

The following are some of the leading photo sharing sites:

- Flickr (`http://flickr.com`)
- Photobucket (`http://photobucket.com`)
- Picasa (`http://picasa.google.com`)
- Pinterest (`http://pinterest.com`)
- SmugMug (`http://smugmug.com`)

Like video sharing, document and presentation sharing can be labor intensive but can also be worth the effort. A great document or slideshow presentation can drive good traffic to your site.

 While you can upload files in variety of formats, typically PDFs work best as they not only maintain their formatting well, but can hold active links, too.

Some more popular document-sharing sites are as follows:

- DocStoc (`http://www.docstoc.com`)
- Issuu (`http://issuu.com`)
- Scribd (`http://scribd.com`)
- Slideshare (`http://slideshare.net`)

 When you set up your bio on your file sharing sites, use the contact information section to add links and descriptive text.

# Social media optimization

Social media has grown to take a significant role in search marketing. Your site should be optimized for social media, making it easy for your site visitors to save, share, and comment on your content. Take advantage of the trends in social interaction as mentioned in the following:

- Make it easy to recommend or share your content on the most popular social networks
- Facilitate bookmarking and tagging
- Provide comment functionality, monitor, and interact

- For rich media, make it easy for others to share it with their friends and site visitors
- Offer subscription functionality, whether by e-mail, RSS, or both

 Joomla! provides several extensions that make it easy for you to add share buttons on your content items. Implement those extensions and make sure the buttons are available on all your content items. See *Chapter 3, Useful Extensions to Enhance SEO,* for a list of suggestions.

As the webmaster of a site, you should make social media part of your content management strategy. One of your goals in content creation is to motivate users to share and recommend the content, thereby extending your site's reach into the users' social circles. Moreover, be proactive: After you add a content item to your site, publicize it via social media channels with links and tags that are consistent with the site's SEO goals.

The use of social channels to drive traffic, combined with the presence of social sharing tools on the site itself, create a push and pull dynamic that will help you leverage your site's contents to the largest number of visitors, creating both inbound links and traffic. Done properly, and backed by compelling content, Social Media Optimization can drive big traffic gains very quickly.

 **Social Media Optimization (SMO)** is not just about creating new links to your content. It is about traffic generation, PR, reputation management, and crisis communications; all of these factors need to be considered in the creation of your SMO strategy.

As a content publisher, you should consider proactive sharing of your content on some, or all of the following:

- Delicious (`http://delicious.com`)
- Digg (`http://digg.com`)
- Facebook (`http://facebook.com`)
- Fark (`http://fark.com`)
- Google + (`http://plus.google.com`)
- Hackernews (`http://hackernews`)
- LinkedIn (`http://linkedin.com`)
- Newsvine (`http://newsvine.com`)

- Pinterest (`http://pinterest.com`)

- Twitter (`http://twitter.com`)

- Reddit (`http://reddit.com`)

- StumbleUpon (`http://stumbleupon.com`)

**Creating profiles**

The past few years have brought a massive proliferation in the number of social media publishing channels. While old standards, such as Technorati and Digg, are still vital, there's a huge number of new channels. How do you decide which of those channels are important to you? How many is too many? The right answer is going to depend on your goals and the time you have to invest in these channels. It's a trade-off, a cost/benefit decision.

At the very least, you should try to maintain profiles (and secure your brand) on all the top channels. Almost all the sites offer you profile pages that you can use to add links back to your primary site and descriptive text. Some, such as Facebook, Google +, and LinkedIn, offer special business-only pages which may be appropriate for your company.

One useful tool to jumpstart channels for profile creation is KnowEm, (`http://knowem.com`), which will search hundreds of the most popular social sites to check the availability of your preferred username. You can then either follow the link they provide and set up your account, or for a small fee, have KnowEm do it for you.

# Reporting and tracking

By definition, SEO is an on-going process. One of the keys to attaining continuous improvement is tracking your efforts. While it does take time to monitor and track, the good news is that there are some great free tools to help you with this.

The most important tool in your SEO tracking toolbox is your web traffic analysis program. Google Analytics is a great choice for filling this role, as it is both free and full-featured. In the final portion of this chapter, we look at the key data points provided by Google Analytics and how that information can help you refine and improve your on-going SEO efforts.

You will also want to look at other, more specific tools, for example, social media tracking tools that help you judge the success of your engagement efforts. There are a number of tools designed to provide feedback on your SMO efforts; which you choose will largely depend on which channels you are using for your social media marketing.

# Popularity metrics

Popularity metrics are yardsticks by which you can judge the relative popularity of your content over time. The primary metrics are as follows:

- Unique visitors
- Visits
- Page views (impressions)
- Average visit length

Let's take a quick look at each of these popularity metrics.

The number of unique visitors is perhaps the most vital statistic, as it counts the visitors to your site while factoring out double counting. Be aware that there are limitations to the counting. The primary impact comes from what are known as "masked IP addresses", that is, networks that automatically give all their users the same IP address. This brings us to an important point: Unique visitors does not count people; it counts computers, and that is the root of the problem. If, for example, two members of a family use the same computer to visit your site one week, you only see one visitor in the number of unique visitors stats.

The visits statistic, on the other hand, gives the total number of visits to your web site during the reporting period. It is a useful metric that will help you arrive at a conclusion regarding the activity trends on your site. Using both the unique visitors and visits metrics, you can run a quick visits-per-visitor calculation as a means of assessing repeat visitors.

Many analytics programs, including Google Analytics, automatically split out repeat visitors and new visitors in the analytics dashboard.

Page views (also called impressions) tells you the total number of pages viewed by site visitors during the reporting period. If visitor A looks at just the home page, but visitor B explores the site, visiting nine pages before leaving, visitors A and B would be collectively responsible for 10 page views. Here again, you will want to look at the average number of page views per visitor. Tracking the trend in this statistic gives you a way of assessing how effective your content is at engaging visitors.

> Forget about "hits". While the term is often used, the metric is of little practical use. Hits simply tell you the number of requests for files received by the server. While this may initially sound good, it falls apart when you consider that a single web page can contain a large number of individual files, each of which is counted and contributes to the total hit count. Unique visitors, views, and page views are much more useful metrics.

The final primary popularity metric is average visit length. Ever wondered if your site is sticky? This statistic and the average pages per visit stat give you a good idea of how sticky your site is. Track this metric across time to assess trend. Content-heavy sites, subscription sites, and sites relying on ad revenues, obsess over this number as it indicates pretty clearly the success of their efforts to draw and hold an audience.

## Traffic source metrics

Where are your visitors coming from? What keywords are bringing them to the site? Look to your analytics reports for answers to these questions. Your Google Analytics dashboard will tell you the sources of traffic, be it search engines or referrals, or even e-mail. Look carefully at the various sources driving traffic.

The search engines section of the analytics reports will also tell you which keyphrases are driving traffic. Look not only at the number of visitors produced by each keyphrase, but also at the amount of time those visitors spend on the site and the number of pages they viewed. This method will give you good insight into whether your content is matching up well with your keyphrase strategy.

Also remember to look at the geographic information in your analytics to assess your progress in your target markets and to discover new markets.

> The referring sites information can be a good source of potential leads for link building.

# e-Business metrics

Measuring the success of your website in terms that are meaningful to management, that is looking for those metrics that are directly relevant to the site's business goals, are what we'll call e-business metrics. This is not a fixed set of indicators common to all sites, but rather a set of indicators that vary according to the nature of the business, its online presence, and the firm's business goals.

There is some common ground here with the popularity metrics discussed previously. The amount of time visitors stay on your site is clearly relevant to whether your site is effective at delivering its message. Of course, this still needs to be tied back to your goals and target markets, and you must take a look at where they are spending the time. In other words, determining the significance of this metric is more involved than simply crunching numbers.

If your firm is concerned with selling advertising space, page views is a key metric for you, as each new page gives you a chance for further ad impressions, which correlates directly to ad revenues.

Conversion rates are a common measure of a business's ability to inspire prospects to take action. While the most common focus is on purchases, conversion rates should not be so narrowly defined. Conversion can also mean registration for a newsletter, download of a product brochure, even participation in a discussion board.

Benchmarking conversion across the site requires you to look at a variety of numbers to get the full picture. For example, if your site provides an option to become a member or sign up for a newsletter, your log files won't give you the clearest picture. Instead, you should count the number of new registrations.

Google Analytics allows you to set up "goals" and "funnels", which put a special emphasis on the users' completion of certain actions, whether it is looking at a page, submitting a form, or placing an order. You can also set values to each goal, allowing you to more easily measure ROI. When creating goals, make sure you mark the end of the process (often a "thank you" or confirmation page), not the beginning or an interim step, else your data will fail to take into account abandonment – that is, people who begin the process but fail to complete it successfully.

Sites focused on online sales should, of course, be tracking the conversion rates as they relate to purchases, but there are also a number of other stats of interest. In addition to the number of purchases, you should at least be tracking the items per purchase and the value of purchases.

Some firms engage in very granular analysis of e-commerce performance and if you wish to really dig into these metrics you will need tools that allow you to slice and dice the data accumulated in your database for each transaction.

Another valuable indicator of e-commerce success is shopping cart abandonment, that is, how many people put items into their shopping cart but then failed to make a purchase. This number should be tracked across time, and consistent efforts must be made to manage this number. A high percentage of abandoned transactions may signal problems with the site's usability or technical glitches that require your attention.

In contrast, if you are not selling online but only marketing your company for offline sales, a key metric for e-business success is leads generated for your sales team. While it is easy to track the number of inquiry e-mails or forms you may receive from your site, it is an incomplete metric. Many people will prefer to contact you directly, rather than submit an online inquiry. In order to track this, your intake process for prospects should include questions about how the prospect found your firm.

In the end, the relevance of particular metrics will vary from firm to firm and you will have to make a decision about what to look at, how often, and how much weight to give it. Data is not the goal, but rather intelligence.

# Link metrics

To track your success gathering inbound links, you will need to look beyond Google Analytics. There are several tools you can use, including your Google and Bing Webmaster accounts. While Google and Bing are free and easy to use (assuming you've already set up the accounts, as we advised in earlier chapters), there is a much better solution: Majestic SEO.

Majestic SEO provides both a free and a premium subscription service. If you control the site you want to track, and have access to the site's root directory on the server, then you can use the free service. Once you have registered, and verified your ownership of the site, you can use Majestic SEO to produce rich reports on the link history of the site. The data is very complete, and allows you to track both internal and external links, to view trends over time, and to look at a variety of other metrics. Visit http://www.majesticseo.com and register to get started.

 Alexa.com also provides a basic link count, but no data on trend, target, or anchor text.

# Summary

This chapter focused on the ongoing work required to conduct an effective and sustained SEO campaign. The key point made in this chapter is that you need to maintain your SEO efforts throughout the life of your site through a combination of techniques.

We looked specifically at link building and social media optimization. Link building was discussed in detail, with an emphasis on how to identify potential link partners and then create and manage a link building campaign. A number of leading sites were identified in a variety of areas.

Social media's increasing role in search marketing was also highlighted, with a recommendation made to not only be proactive about using social media to promote your content but also to inspire and motivate your users to promote your content through their social networks.

In the final part of this chapter, we discussed the importance of monitoring your progress, and feeding the data back into your efforts in order to attain continuous refinement and improvement in your SEO efforts. The emphasis was on how to use the key metrics you can find in Google Analytics, but the information is relevant to any web traffic monitoring program.

# Index

## T

**third party services, SEO**
  setting up  70
**third party tools**
  Bing Webmaster Tools  70
  Google Analytics  70
  Google Webmaster Tools  70
**tips, title tag  30**
**title attributes**  52
**title tag**
  article title vs. page title  31-34
  configuring  28-30
  tips  30
**traffic source metrics**  90
**Trellian KW Discovery tool**
  URL  62
**Twitter**
  URL  88

## U

**Ubersuggest**
  URL  62
**Ultimate Site Tools**  47
**unique visitors, popularity metrics**  89
**URL aliases**
  configuring  25, 26
  creating, for articles  26, 28

## V

**variants**  67
**Veoh**
  URL  85
**video and file sharing**  85

**video and file sharing sites**
  DailyMotion  85
  MetaCafe  85
  PhotoBucket  85
  Veoh  85
  YouTube  85
**Vimeo**
  URL  85
**visits statistic, popularity metrics**  89

## W

**WebWire**
  URL  85
**White hat**  17
**WordStream**
  URL  62
**WordTracker**
  URL  62

## X

**Xmap**  47
**XML site maps**
  about  17, 50
  setting up  51, 52

## Thank you for buying
# Joomla! Search Engine Optimization

# About Packt Publishing

Packt, pronounced 'packed', published its first book "*Mastering phpMyAdmin for Effective MySQL Management*" in April 2004 and subsequently continued to specialize in publishing highly focused books on specific technologies and solutions.

Our books and publications share the experiences of your fellow IT professionals in adapting and customizing today's systems, applications, and frameworks. Our solution based books give you the knowledge and power to customize the software and technologies you're using to get the job done. Packt books are more specific and less general than the IT books you have seen in the past. Our unique business model allows us to bring you more focused information, giving you more of what you need to know, and less of what you don't.

Packt is a modern, yet unique publishing company, which focuses on producing quality, cutting-edge books for communities of developers, administrators, and newbies alike. For more information, please visit our website: www.packtpub.com.

# About Packt Open Source

In 2010, Packt launched two new brands, Packt Open Source and Packt Enterprise, in order to continue its focus on specialization. This book is part of the Packt Open Source brand, home to books published on software built around Open Source licences, and offering information to anybody from advanced developers to budding web designers. The Open Source brand also runs Packt's Open Source Royalty Scheme, by which Packt gives a royalty to each Open Source project about whose software a book is sold.

# Writing for Packt

We welcome all inquiries from people who are interested in authoring. Book proposals should be sent to author@packtpub.com. If your book idea is still at an early stage and you would like to discuss it first before writing a formal book proposal, contact us; one of our commissioning editors will get in touch with you.

We're not just looking for published authors; if you have strong technical skills but no writing experience, our experienced editors can help you develop a writing career, or simply get some additional reward for your expertise.

## Joomla! Mobile Development Beginner's Guide

ISBN: 978-1-84951-708-9          Paperback: 288 pages

Build Joomla! Websites for mobile devices

1. Step by step approach to build efficient mobile websites with Joomla!

2. Learn everything from organizing your content to completely changing the site's look and feel

3. Friendly, clear instructions and explanations enriched with the necessary screenshots

## Joomla! 2.5 Beginner's Guide

ISBN: 978-1-84951-790-4          Paperback: 426 pages

As easy to use step-by-step guide to creating perfect websites with the free Joomla! CMS

1. Create a Joomla! website in an hour with the help of easy-to-follow steps and screenshots.

2. Go beyond a typical Joomla! site to make a website that meets your specific needs.

3. Learn how to secure, administrate, and fill your site with content.

4. Update to the popular Joomla! 1.5 Beginner's Guide by Eric Tiggeler.

Please check **www.PacktPub.com** for information on our titles

## Joomla! VirtueMart 1.1 Theme and Template Design

ISBN: 978-1-84951-454-5        Paperback: 384 pages

Give a unique look and feel to your VirtueMart
e-commerce store

1.  Thorough discussion of template structure,
    available fields, and customization possibilities

2.  More than 50 real-world exercises that can be
    directly adapted to your store

3.  A comprehensive reference to all templates in
    the VirtueMart default theme including usage
    of each template and all available fields

4.  Integrate with existing Joomla! plugins and
    JavaScript frameworks

## ChronoForms 3.1 for Joomla! site Cookbook

ISBN: 978-1-84951-062-2        Paperback: 376 pages

80 recipes for building attractive and interactive
Joomla! forms

1.  Develop feature-rich Joomla! forms with
    the help of easy-to-follow steps and ample
    screenshots

2.  Publish forms, that let you interact with your
    users, to a website using ChronoForms in
    minutes, not in hours

3.  Explore the versatility of ChronoForms and use
    them to make your web site an interactive one

Please check **www.PacktPub.com** for information on our titles